Praise for

UNLEARN

"To succeed, it's critical for everyone, from executives to entrepreneurs, to know how to let go of behavior and methods that have helped them achieve in the past but are now limiting. *Unlearn* explains how to enter into a continuous cycle of replacing old ideas and models with new ones in order to adapt in an ever-changing world. Founded on clear principles and filled with stories from the field, it advocates for courage over comfort not just now, but in whatever circumstances the future offers up."

—ERIC RIES, Founder, Long-Term Stock Exchange,
and author of *The Startup Way* and *The Lean Startup*

"Surprisingly, many of the attributes that enabled small companies to scale into large ones are now the very things that impede their future prospects. Some telltale signs of trouble include administration replacing true leadership, process morphing into bureaucracy and red tape, and past successes inhibiting the ability to drive needed change. All this leads to a culture that sacrifices speed, client centricity, and innovation. Successful companies are mission driven and customer and employee obsessed, and they passionately preserve the founding mission of the organization while having the humility to unlearn the tried-and-true ways of the past. This book is an essential reminder that the ability to unlearn is an enduring core competency of extraordinary individuals—and the winning organizations they lead."

—JOHN MARCANTE, CIO, Vanguard

"Many executives and entrepreneurs hang on to thinking and methods that were once useful, but may limit their future success. Apply the lessons in *Unlearn* and unlock the full potential in yourself, your teams, and your organization."

—NOELLE EDER, Chief Information and Digital Officer, Hilton

"The only thing that is constant is change. And it's happening faster and faster. Disruption is ongoing, yet leaders tend to think incrementally about the future. Barry shows us a better way: the only way to disrupt yourself before someone does it for you is to unlearn, separate yourself from what has worked in the past in order to create an open space to shape the future. A great read for any leader in fast-moving environments faced with the realization that what worked in the past won't work in the future."

—STEPHANE KASRIEL, CEO, Upwork, and Co-Chair, Future Council in Education, Gender and Work, Global World Economic Forum

"We work in a world of complexity, revolutionary technologies, and dynamic change. The only advantage is people—people who are engaged and can rapidly learn and unlearn. That's why I love Barry O'Reilly's new book, *Unlearn*. It correctly magnifies a vital and often overlooked concept, the importance of unlearning for organizational success. Typically, organizations lose capability and innovation by their inability to unlearn ideas that are no longer relevant. This book provides guidance on the steps to take to form a culture of learning and unlearning."

—EDWARD J. HOFFMAN, PhD, former Chief Knowledge Officer, NASA, and Academic Director, Information and Knowledge Strategy, Columbia University

"*Unlearn* lays out an easy-to-use system to constantly challenge what we think we know. Barry draws from a wealth of relevant and relatable examples to help us better understand how we can apply the powerful principles in our own lives. Reading *Unlearn* inspired me to challenge many of my own old mindsets and ideals, and I've seen a considerable improvement in my own results and outcomes. Inspiring work!"

—STEPHEN ORBAN, General Manager, New Initiative, Amazon Web Services, and author of *Ahead in the Cloud*

"The only way to thrive in a world of accelerating change driven by exponential technologies is through adaptability and continuous learning. Barry

O'Reilly has identified the critical first step: unlearning the past. *Unlearn* is a methodical playbook for breaking ourselves away from the anchors of the past and accelerating into the future."

—ROB NAIL, Associate Founder and CEO, Singularity University

"When you work at the intersection of technology, design, and people, change is constant, and unlearning what brought individuals and teams success in the past is of critical importance for future success. Today, every industry is changing rapidly, and the ability to learn and unlearn is a major factor differentiating the highest-performing companies and individuals from those that are falling behind. Barry O'Reilly's book, *Unlearn*, with its experience-based framework, is inspiring and essential reading for all of us in leadership positions, especially within traditional industries."

—KATRI HARRA-SALONEN, Chief Digital Officer, Finnair

"Part of unlearning is not getting stuck doing only what worked in the past. When 97 percent of people think you should just go back to doing what you've been doing, or resist the change that you are trying to make, you know you're on to something, and that's where the breakthrough journey begins."

—STEPHEN SCOTT, Chief Digital Officer, Avios Group Limited

"The best way to master our ever-changing business environment is by designing—and redesigning—our deep-seated habits and routines. In *Unlearn*, Barry O'Reilly explains in an easy-to-understand way how to introduce new habits into your workplace intentionally and systematically. By unlearning old habits and welcoming new routines, you have the unique opportunity to create a fast path to extraordinary results. The process Barry outlines draws on key methods from my work in behavior design, as well as techniques from my Tiny Habits® method. In writing this book for business leaders in every industry, Barry offers a step-by-step framework for unlocking untapped potential in your company—and in yourself."

—BJ FOGG, PhD, behavior scientist and
creator of Tiny Habits® method

"Barry has done it again! Leveraging his work with some of today's most innovative and successful companies, Barry has delivered the primer on digital transformation. *Unlearn* focuses on the trickiest and least-obvious starting point: unlearning the habits that trap leaders and companies in past successes that no longer deliver results today. This step-by-step guide to gaining fresh perspectives provides clear and highly actionable advice on how to stimulate and incubate successful innovation throughout the enterprise, enabling breakthrough performance."

—JODY MULKEY, CTO, Ticketmaster

"In a world where the pace of change is so fast, it is difficult to keep up, leaders often unknowingly get in their own way. To stay competitive, they must build the skills to continuously evolve and embrace the unknown. *Unlearn* provides a structured framework to help individuals and the organizations they lead adapt to the changing times by unlearning and then relearning the skills to help themselves break through and stay competitive. It will get everyone on the road to lifelong learning in a safe and systematic way."

—RESHMA SHAIKH, VP Strategy and Operations,
Office of the COO, Springer Nature

"Barry's book plays a key role in my assignment—leading a large enterprise through digital transformation—not only on a personal level but especially on an entrepreneurial level. Unlearn is a universally applicable principle for successful transformation. A must-read for business leaders."

—NILS STAMM, Chief Digital Officer, Deutschland Telekom,
and Board Member, Münchner Kreis

"We are living through an unprecedented period of disruption. The challenge for many organizations and individuals is how to move from their current landscape to a new landscape without any guide. Many are falling back on outdated business models and processes that are not delivering the outcomes they hoped for. This book presents an alternative view that begins with unlearning the old and adapting to what is required for the future."

—JORA GILL, Chief Digital Officer, *The Economist*

"We have all been there: that feeling of facing challenging obstacles, environments, and circumstances, but knowing we must do something to overcome. Transforming big organizations starts small, by transforming ourselves. Barry O'Reilly challenges us all to unlearn and innovate our own game. In this comprehensive and insightful book, he provides an actionable framework to help us to unlearn, do things differently, and win."

—LEA HICKMAN, Partner, Silicon Valley Product Group,
and former VP of Product Management, Adobe

"So many organizations are rooted in what has made them successful in the past that it is difficult for them to explore new approaches. This institutional knowledge becomes so ingrained that transformation almost becomes impossible. *Unlearn* is a great reminder to leaders that we need to face the future versus dwelling on the past. With a world that is constantly changing, unlearning becomes a critical tool for holding teams accountable for their future strategy and growth."

—ANDREW MEYER, Director, NHS Digital

"We have all seen industry titans fall due to their inability to change and adapt to what is happening around them. They all saw exactly what was going on, but were locked in their past behaviors and ways of operating. In *Unlearn*, Barry provides real-world examples of how leaders can avoid this trap and redefine how they operate. The book provides very practical steps on how to unlearn what has made us all successful in the past and relearn new ways of thinking and working. It is a must-read for anyone who wants to help themselves and their companies stay ahead of their competitors in a fast, ever-changing environment."

—JEFF REIHL, EVP and Chief Technology Officer, LexisNexis

"In fast-paced digital environments, we constantly need to innovate and think differently to drive growth. By applying the three steps—unlearn, relearn, and break through—you can let go of old approaches that may no longer drive success, unlearn old behaviors, and adapt to your situation to achieve extraordinary results. Barry provides relevant examples that bring the system of unlearning to life with tools to apply both in business and your everyday life."

—SARAH BARTLETT, former CMO, Time Out Group, lastminute.com, and Travelocity International

"History has shown us that past performance does not guarantee future success. Barry reminds us how important it is to challenge our assumptions, continuously seek new information and different perspectives, and decide what to unlearn. We can all look back at examples where we were held back by what we believed to be true, selecting data and input that validated our opinion and hypotheses, rather than deliberately seeking that which may challenge us. The skill to unlearn knows no organizational or role boundaries. A great read for anyone who seeks to flourish in our world of perpetual change, and break through the repeated cycle of stifled innovation."

—JENN BENNETT, Technical Director, Office of the CTO, Google Cloud

"You don't add innovation to a business; you get out of its way. To do that, you need to unlearn all the accumulated cruft that's slowing you down. This book will guide you and help you make the case."

—ADRIAN COCKCROFT,
Cloud computing pioneer

"I believe in the truism that 'conventional thinking tends to yield conventional results.' In that light, Barry O'Reilly is an unconventional thinker and *Unlearn* is the extraordinary result. If you are a business leader striving to hit hypergrowth or do something significant, you should read this book as a toolkit for unconstraining your thinking and pushing yourself, your team, and your company to reach new heights."

—BREANDEN BENESCHOTT, Cofounder and COO, Toptal

"Barry's innovative system highlights the importance for both individuals and the organizations they lead to unlearn once useful practices that have become inhibiting and limit their future success in the new (and ever-evolving) paradigms in which they operate."

—TERREN PETERSON, VP of Cyber Security, Capital One

"*Unlearn* is compelling, whether you are an executive trying to move your organization to the next level or simply interested in better understanding how to unlock your own potential. The concepts in *Unlearn* make complete sense. They seem almost obvious. Yet it pushes us way outside of our comfort zone and shows us how to do this systematically. Barry provides a powerful system to break down the principles of unlearning and put them back together using pragmatic techniques that feel doable. *Unlearn* isn't just intellectually stimulating; it is essential for anyone wanting to understand and surpass the maximum we all hit at some point—in a project, in a career, in our life."

—JEROME BONHOMME,
CTO and EVP, American Specialty Health

"When we look at our life clutter, we can easily understand that purging stuff we don't need helps make room for what's important. The same can be said for our learning. Yet we often find it hard to let go of our habits, at times even to the detriment of our own future success. Barry's book guides us through identifying how to unlearn our past habits so that we can relearn new ways of thinking and accomplishing our goals. I highly recommend this book for anyone experiencing or leading structural changes in their workplace."

—THANIYA KEEREEPART, Head of Mobile and Platforms, TED

"Operating effectively in a global and increasingly decentralized world means unlearning old behaviors, biases, and gut instincts. Our challenge is to be more aware, experimental, and open to change. *Unlearn* is an outstanding read, and reminds us that change, feeling comfortable with being uncomfortable, and learning through trying new things is the best way to build new behavior and improve the way we work together."

—RON GARRETT, Founding Partner, ConsenSys Labs

"The magic of this book is how it shows that growth, change, and progress come not from learning more but from unlearning that which restricts us, keeps us in our comfort zone, and ultimately, sidetracks innovation and our own careers. This book shows you the way forward."

—JACK TATAR, bestselling coauthor of
Cryptoassets: The Innovative Investor's Guide to Bitcoin and Beyond

"Gosh, how I wish that I had access to a book like this at the beginning of my career. Now I know why my leadership behaviors, style, and even biases can hold me back. Learning to unlearn teaches you how to be productive, avoid psychological barriers, and pivot quickly by using new mental models in order to power your career development, improve your social interactions, and really help you to enjoy your work."

—FIN GOULDING, International CIO, Aviva, and
coauthor of *Flow: A Handbook for Change-Makers,
Mavericks, Innovation Activists, and Leaders*

"I've spent 20 years in the business of IT trying to make the cultural shift that propels great leaders forward. Barry's book provides the tools to break down the aging perceptions of leadership and cut to the heart of what works. *Unlearn* sheds the comforts of conformity and delivers the framework for evolving and growing with each and every challenge. Innovation and transformation are the products of our willingness to seek out the change both we as leaders and the business need to be successful."

—AARON GETTE, CIO, The Bay Clubs

"*Unlearn* is a powerful gem that offers a practical way to deepen innovation and achieve outstanding performance on all fronts. The three-step model— unlearn, relearn, break through—is a crucial system for success that's both easy to digest and easy to execute. Want to perform at top levels? You need the ability to unlearn and Barry O'Reilly shows you how!"

—**KAREN MARTIN,** President, The Karen Martin Group, Inc., and author of *Clarity First* and the Shingo Award–winning *The Outstanding Organization* and *Value Stream Mapping*

"We all want to work smarter, but Barry O'Reilly offers a powerful mindset shift: You can't just add new techniques—you must also consciously destroy the often-invisible habits that are tripping you up. Unlearning is a powerful concept, but what I love about this book is that it's not just one concept, it's a master course in leadership that efficiently synthesizes many of the best books and practices in the business world. *Unlearn* is like 30 great books in one."

—**JAKE KNAPP,** bestselling author of *Sprint* and *Make Time*

"Simple and obvious changes are not always easy, and obvious is in the eye of the beholder. I'm fond of saying you haven't learned anything until you change behaviors, but the impediments to change are often anchored in our past success and our current identity. What we do is who we are. Unlearning solves this problem with a feedback loop revisiting assumptions about what we do and why. The most profound progress rarely comes from adding more but from removing the unnecessary and the useless. If we want to be more in the future, we need to unlearn what holds us back today. Filled with relatable anecdotes and real-world examples, unlearning provides an actionable model while being accessible and fun to read."

—**ANDREW CLAY SHAFER,** Senior Director of Technology, Pivotal; Cofounder, Puppet; Core Organizer, DevOpsDays; and author of *Web Operations: Agile Infrastructure*

"Barry provides an actionable system for unlearning successful habits of the past that are hobbling leaders and organizations from dealing with today's challenges."

—**CHIVAS NAMBIAR,** Executive Director, Cloud and Platform Engineering, Verizon

"Barry hits on a key element of learning that's easy to overlook. We can't just add new knowledge to our repertoire. We have to take the time to examine what's no longer working for us and unlearn those patterns and behaviors, before we can learn new patterns and behaviors. Barry provides a crisp and clear model to help leaders do exactly that. *Unlearn* is a must-read for growth-minded professionals."

—TERESA TORRES, Founder and
Product Discovery Coach, Product Talk

"Barry's message for leaders is simple and understated, but contains deep truths about innovation and growth. Sometimes the best way forward is a step back."

—JOSH SEIDEN, coauthor of *Sense & Respond* and *Lean UX*

"So many times our teams, leaders, and cultures resist new ideas—not because they don't inherently believe in them but because they force us to behave in ways that conflict with 'the way we've always done things.' This, more than any other issue, is the reason organizations struggle to evolve and survive. Amazingly, this is exactly what this book tackles head-on to ensure that you and your teams unlearn the behaviors that keep you from your true potential."

—JEFF GOTHELF, coauthor of *Sense & Respond* and *Lean UX*

"*Unlearn* is a must-read for every leader who is looking to grow. This book gets deep into the core of where people—and the organizations they lead—fail to adapt to new situational realities and transform. It's not just about learning new ways of working, but effectively unlearning our outdated habits that limit our mindset and actions, so that we can thrive in the face of uncertainty as we build the future."

—MELISSA PERRI, CEO, Produx Labs, and author of *The Build Trap*

"The new competitive advantage is not learning faster than your competition, but rapidly putting that learning into action. Barry's book is the definitive guide on how to do exactly that."

—DAVID J. BLAND, Founder, Precoil,
and author of *Testing Business Ideas*

"This is the book you need when you realize that doing what you've always done isn't enough anymore."

—JONNY SCHNEIDER, Principal, ThoughtWorks, and
author of *Understanding Design Thinking, Lean, and Agile*

"Being able to unlearn bad old habits and embrace new ways of thinking and doing is undoubtedly the key skill of the millennium, and in this book Barry gives us all the blueprint for how to do it and succeed in the future."

—MARTIN ERIKKSON, Cofounder of Mind the Product
and coauthor of *Product Leadership*

UNLEARN

LET GO OF PAST SUCCESS TO ACHIEVE
EXTRAORDINARY RESULTS

BARRY O'REILLY

Mc
Graw
Hill
Education

New York Chicago San Francisco Athens London Madrid
Mexico City Milan New Delhi Singapore Sydney Toronto

1 2 3 4 5 6 7 8 9   QVS   23 22 21 20 19 18

ISBN   978-1-260-14301-0
MHID   1-260-14301-5

e-ISBN   978-1-260-14302-7
e-MHID   1-260-14302-3

Library of Congress Cataloging-in-Publication Data

Names: O'Reilly, Barry (Business consultant), author.
Title: Unlearn : let go of past success to achieve extraordinary results / Barry O'Reilly.
Description: New York : McGraw-Hill, [2019] | Includes bibliographical references.
Identifiers: LCCN 2018039325 | ISBN 9781260143010 (alk. paper) | ISBN 1260143015
Subjects: LCSH: Organizational change. | Organizational learning. | Success in business.
Classification: LCC HD58.8 .O66 2019 | DDC 658.3/124—dc23 LC record available at https://lccn.loc.gov/2018039325

McGraw-Hill Education products are available at special quantity discounts to use as premiums and sales promotions or for use in corporate training programs. To contact a representative, please visit the Contact Us pages at www.mhprofessional.com.

To Qiu Yi

For encouraging and challenging me to unlearn many of the beliefs and behaviors that have held me back, and relearn how to achieve much more than I believed possible of myself. I look forward to the endless breakthroughs you and I will continue to discover, together.

Contents

Introduction
The Remarkable Power of Unlearning

If you're always trying to be normal, you will
never know how amazing you can be.
—*Maya Angelou*

At the beginning of the 2010 season, tennis superstar Serena Williams was at the pinnacle of her sport. She was the number-1 ranked woman tennis player in the world. However, while dining at a Munich restaurant, Serena accidently stepped on some broken glass. The next day, and 18 stitches later, she played in an exhibition match but was forced to the sidelines for the rest of the season. She finished the year ranked number 4 on the women's professional tennis circuit.

After sitting out the first half of 2011 as she recovered from the foot injury (along with a pulmonary embolism and hematoma), Serena went back to work. While her singles record for the year was 22 wins and just 3 losses, which included a fourth-round defeat at Wimbledon and a straight-set thrashing in the final round of the US Open, she had to skip both the Australian and French Opens. She ended the year ranked number 12.

Surely, these results were nothing more than temporary setbacks, yet Serena's slide continued. In 2012, she lost to 56th-ranked Ekaterina Makarova in the fourth round of the Australian Open. But it was at the French Open, the second Grand Slam event of the season, where everything fell apart completely. Serena lost to 111th-ranked Virginie Razzano in the first round, the first time in her entire career that she was defeated in the opening round of a Grand Slam match. The *New York Times* described the defeat as "an upset that ranked among the most stunning and unexpected in the recent history of the French Open . . ."[1]

Doubts filled Serena's head, and they impacted her performance. She was doing everything she had been doing in the past—she trained longer, worked harder, and her preparation was perfect—but what had brought her success in the past was no longer working, and she was no longer winning.

Why *weren't* her tried-and-trusted methods working?

Why *wasn't* she winning?

Was her time at the top *up*?

There comes a time in the life of every individual when doing the things that brought you success in the past no longer delivers the same results. You wake up, walk into your office, and sit at your desk just as you always have. But suddenly you're stuck, stagnating, unsatisfied, or struggling with what was once your secret to success. You might find yourself asking:

Why am I not living up to my expectations?

Why can't I solve this problem?

Why do I constantly avoid taking on this particular challenge?

The world evolves, conditions change, and new norms emerge. Instead of adapting, people find themselves stuck in their patterns of thinking and behaving. Most don't realize the new situational reality until it bites.

This is the paradox of success. While thinking and doing certain methods may have brought you success in the past, it's almost certain they won't continue to bring you success in the future. The key is to recognize the signals and break through before it's too late. Your once-successful strategies can cause your downfall. The challenge is to make the adjustments and adapt, not get caught in the past.

But how?

My inspiration to write *Unlearn* came from what I frequently find to be a significant inhibitor when helping high-performance individuals get better—not the ability to learn new things but the inability to unlearn mindsets, behaviors, and methods that were once effective but now limit their success.

Highly effective leaders are constantly searching for inspiration and for new ideas. But before any real breakthroughs can happen, we need to step away from the old models, mindsets, and behaviors that are limiting our potential and current performance. We must unlearn what brought us success in the past to find continued success in the future.

In the pages that follow, I share how the Cycle of Unlearning is a new way of thinking and a new way of leading organizations in every industry. It's not difficult to learn more. What is difficult is to know what to *unlearn*, what to stop, and what to throw away. That is the focus of this book.

I believe we can all grow, have impact, and achieve extraordinary results—I've seen it time and time again. Outstanding individuals achieve success not by chance and not by luck, but by continuously and routinely applying a system of *unlearning*—sometimes intentionally, often unintentionally. My aspiration is to give this superpower to you.

I define *unlearning* as the process of letting go of, moving away from, and reframing once-useful mindsets and acquired behaviors that were effective in the past, but now limit our success. It's not forgetting or discarding knowledge or experience; it's the conscious act of letting go of outdated information and actively gathering and taking in new information to inform effective decision making and action.

Unlearning is an essential yet often overlooked step to being able to learn. While most people agree that we struggle to adopt new techniques to improve, fewer recognize that our existing knowledge and know-how can inhibit us further. Not all learning is unquestionably beneficial. We can learn the wrong lessons, bad habits, and flawed or once-useful ideas that are now obsolete. Unlearning our thinking and behavior can be harder than learning it in the first place.

In this book, we'll dig deep into the practice of unlearning—what it is, why you should adopt it, and how you can leverage its tremendous power for yourself, your teams, and your organization. If you already feel you've unlearned before, great—I'll teach you how to do it intentionally. If not, I'll teach you to practice it deliberately.

I'll show you how to think big but start small, and why choosing courage over comfort can take you to places you never imagined possible. You'll see how tackling uncertainty can lead you to exponential growth and impact, and I will provide you with a proven system for unlearning what brought you success in the past (but no longer does), and then relearn what you need to achieve endless breakthroughs in your future.

Let's get started.

1

Why Unlearn?

You must unlearn what you have learned.
—Yoda

A
s Serena Williams assessed her devastating string of losses on the court, she feared she might be nearing the end of her fabled career. In 2012, the average age for women Grand Slam tournament players was just 24 years old.[1] Serena was almost 31 years old, she had been a professional tennis player for half her life, and she hadn't won a Grand Slam event in two years. The trend was not a positive one.

It had been a good run, but according to reports in the media, Serena wanted to win just one more Grand Slam tournament before her career was over for good.[2] She had very clear aspirations, but she wasn't living up to them. It was time to stop letting fear hold her back, and instead focus on the outcome she wanted to achieve—to win again. "I decided I was going to die trying," she said. "I just had to go back on court, no matter what. It would have been weird if I hadn't tried."[3]

That one last shot came from a very unlikely place, remarkably, and from the most unlikely of sources.

Immediately after her devastating loss at the French Open, Serena looked for a court in Paris where she could practice and unwind. She found her way to a tennis academy for juniors owned and run by Patrick Mouratoglou, who also served as a coach there. While Mouratoglou had coached a handful of mid-ranked players—he was then coaching 37th-ranked men's player Grigor Dimitrov—he didn't come from a classic coaching background, and he had never before coached a player of Serena's caliber.

Patrick's father had founded EDF Énergies Nouvelles, a renewable energy company that made him one of the richest men in France. At age 15, Patrick was a middle-rung junior player with dreams of turning pro, but his parents insisted that he instead focus on his studies so that he would one day be able to step into his father's shoes at EDF. Patrick complied with his parents' wishes. He quit tennis, doubled down on his studies, and eventually took a position at EDF Énergies Nouvelles, where he learned the ins and outs of business and leadership.

However, the siren song of tennis continued to beckon, and at age 26, Patrick quit the family business to open his own youth tennis academy. Says Mouratoglou about the difficult conversation he had with his father, "I told him, 'I'm sorry. It is interesting, but it's not a passion for me, and I need passion in my life—I really need my freedom.'"[4]

Serena arrived at Mouratoglou's academy, and Patrick watched her practice for 45 minutes. After observing how she moved around the court, how she hit the ball, how she served and volleyed, he gave Serena his unvarnished feedback. "Every time you hit, you're off balance, which makes you miss a lot," he told her. "Also, you lose power because [your] body weight doesn't go through [the shots], and you're not moving up, so your game is slow."[5]

She was curious about Patrick's insights and said. "Let's work on it."[6] And that's exactly what they did. The pair trained together every day for the rest of the week, and then Serena returned home to the United States to prepare for Wimbledon.

Just days before the Wimbledon tournament was set to begin, Serena made the decision to take on relatively unproven Frenchman Patrick Mouratoglou as her coach. He would step into the role that her father, Richard Williams, had filled for both Serena and her sister Venus from the time they first held tennis racquets in their hands. What followed was truly extraordinary.

Serena won her next 19 matches and took Wimbledon and the US Open, along with a gold medal at the 2012 Summer Olympics (defeating Maria Sharapova in straight sets) and the season-closing WTA Tour Championships, trouncing Sharapova (again, in straight sets). She ended the season the number-three woman tennis player in the world.

Serena Williams was back, with a vengeance.

When Serena decided to make the coaching switch from her father to Patrick Mouratoglou, she was taking a huge risk. In the world of tennis coaching, which emphasized molding players to a rigid standard set by the coach, Mouratoglou's methods were seen as too unconventional, even radical. Patrick learned skills from the time he spent in his father's business, and then adapted and applied them to his coaching. He took a holistic approach to coaching, not just the game but the mindset and mentality—what many people highlight now as one of Serena's greatest strengths.

In Patrick's words:

> My goal has always been to enable every player to maximize his potential through individualized training. My method consists in being able to connect with your player . . . I don't believe in a method that would fit everyone but more in one that is based on being able to build a personalized plan for each player that will lead him/her to success. My job is about adaptation and not about repeating a [one-size-fits-all] pattern.[7]

Both Williams and Mouratoglou were out of their comfort zones, but this was necessary to find the breakthrough in her game. They both had something to prove, a purpose that drove them. Serena wanted to show the world she wasn't done—that she could win another Grand Slam—and Patrick wanted to prove to the tennis establishment that it was wrong about his coaching methods. If the partnership failed,

Williams's career could have very well ended with retirement and Mouratoglou would have returned to the relative obscurity of his youth tennis academy, both chastened by an experiment gone wrong in a very public way.

Choosing Patrick put Serena squarely in an unfamiliar, unknown, and uncertain situation. She knew exactly what to expect from her father as her lifelong coach, but not from Mouratoglou, whom she had personally known for only a few weeks before she made the decision to hire him. But Serena knew it was time to let go and move away from what she always had previously done in search of improved performance—and one last Grand Slam win.

With Mouratoglou's help, Serena Williams began the process of unlearning the methods that were no longer bringing her the success she so desperately wanted, while relearning new techniques and tactics on the court—leading to breakthroughs in her performance.

They thought big (one last Grand Slam win) but started small, introducing a few tiny tweaks to existing routines—nothing major—such as working on speeding up Serena's footwork so that she could set up for shots and hit the ball earlier. As each small step showed signs of progress, the trust between them grew stronger with each passing day. This gave Serena the confidence she needed to move away from the comfort and certainty of her tried-and-trusted methods and tackle new challenges and win.

In addition, Patrick helped Serena see the blind spots in her game that she was unaware of, sparking new perspectives, new thinking, and new behaviors. He convinced Serena, for example, of the importance of pre-match preparation, including analyzing each of her opponents, exploring probable game scenarios, and developing tactics to be used during the course of her match. According to Mouratoglou, "The more information you have, the more you are ready to play against them." But, as he points out, "I don't know if she believed in [this approach] before or not, but she was not doing it."[8]

Serena listened to the advice of her coach, and she adapted her approach to the game—taking small steps and introducing new behaviors. Says Mouratoglou about Serena's drive to keep shaking up her game, "She hates to do the same things all the time. She's a person who loves to learn and loves to progress, and it's very important to add new things to her game."[9] In short, Serena unlearned, relearned, and then experienced breakthroughs—again and again—leading her to higher and higher performance.

Each breakthrough developed deeper resilience in Serena's mind, reinforcing the strong belief she had in her ability to come back from difficult and losing positions time and time again. She developed a system to unlearn what was holding her back and win when she most needed to. According to tennis performance psychologist, Jim Loehr, it's clear to Serena's opponents when she is ready to come back from behind and win. Says Loehr, "All of a sudden she walks differently, she acts differently, and her opponent knows it's over."[10]

Serena's deep well of resilience also equates to extraordinary results. When women tennis players lose the opening set, they have on average only a 25 percent chance of coming back to win.[11] When Serena loses the first set of a match, however, she's almost as likely to win the match as she is to lose it. She's 90-92 in her career when dropping the first set—almost double the statistical probability of a comeback succeeding. Better still, if a match goes the distance to three sets, Serena wins more than 70 percent of the time, posting a 150-59 record.[12]

During the course of the 2002–2003 seasons, Serena held all four Grand Slam singles titles simultaneously, making her one of only a very small handful of tennis players in history to achieve this feat—labeled the "Serena Slam" by the media. After bouncing back from her defeat at the French Open in 2012, Serena thought bigger, and set her sights on an even more audacious aspiration, a second Serena Slam. This became her new purpose, and she achieved it during the 2014–2015 season—12 years after her first—becoming the only person ever to do so twice.

At her side? Coach Patrick Mouratoglou. Said Serena, "After I won my first Grand Slam with Patrick in 2012, I knew my life and my career had changed. At the 2017 Australian Open we broke the record by winning my twenty-third major—our tenth Grand Slam title together. Twenty-three is just the start of us. As he told me, why limit myself?"[13]

Since losing in that first round in Paris, and working with Patrick Mouratoglou, Serena Williams has made it to the finals in 14 of the 22 Grand Slam tournaments in which she has participated,* winning 10 of them—the 2017 Australian Open while eight weeks pregnant![14] It's no wonder many consider Serena to be not just the best woman tennis player in the history of the sport, but the best tennis player *period.*

While they may not be as accomplished on the court as Serena Williams, leaders, executives, managers, teams, and businesses often face the same situation Serena did—a point at which doing the things that brought them success in the past no longer work. To succeed, they must unlearn, relearn, and break through.

This is the heart of my unlearning system, and in the next chapter, you'll discover how it can help you break through the barriers that hold you back to achieve the extraordinary results you seek in every aspect of your work and life.

Unlearning the Unlearned

While we consider the idea of unlearning in a business context, it is something that permeates our lives—and human history—perhaps without us even realizing it.

About 2,000 years ago, the Roman Empire ruled the Western world. During its prime, it stretched from the capital of Rome (at the time, the largest city in the world) to present-day England in the north, North Africa in the south, and west and east through much of Europe and the Middle East. It occupied more than 1.9 million square miles and included approximately 20 percent of the world's population. For almost

---

* Valid to 2018.

500 years, the Roman Empire was the greatest military, economic, and cultural power the earth had ever seen.

For centuries, scholars have mused over what it was that brought the Romans such tremendous success. Was it the empire's visionary leaders? Its prime location on the Tiber River? A happy confluence of historical events? Perhaps not. In 1734, French political philosopher Baron de Montesquieu explained that the Roman Empire's success could in great part be traced to its unique ability to adapt to new circumstances in its environment by unlearning what had brought it success in the past. According to Montesquieu:

> It should be noted that the main reason for the Romans becoming masters of the world was that, having fought successively against all peoples, they always gave up their own practices as soon as they found better ones.[15]

So as you see, unlearning has been with us for a very long time, as have the benefits unlearning provides. There was much scientific research done on the topic of unlearning in the 1980s and '90s. Ironically, however, we seem to have unlearned it!

Beginning in the 1980s, research interest in a concept called the *learning organization* gained momentum. Building a learning organization—in which employees and the organization itself could learn more at a greater velocity—was seen as an important competitive advantage in a global economy that was increasingly knowledge-based. The idea of the learning organization exploded into the mainstream with the publication of Peter Senge's seminal book, *The Fifth Discipline: The Art and Practice of the Learning Organization*, in 1990.

In his book, Senge presented what he termed the Laws of Systems Thinking:

1. Today's problems come from yesterday's "solutions."
2. The harder you push, the harder the system pushes back.

3. Behavior grows better before it grows worse.
4. The easy way out usually leads back in.
5. The cure can be worse than the disease.
6. Faster is slower.
7. Cause and effect are not closely related in time and space.
8. Small changes can produce big results—but the areas of highest leverage are often the least obvious.
9. You can have your cake and eat it too—but not at once.
10. Dividing an elephant in half does not produce two small elephants.
11. There is no blame.[16]

Lifelong learning was assumed to be necessary for high-performance people and organizations. And so, while American business executives and managers jumped on the learning organization bandwagon in droves, researchers found that there was a related concept that needed to be considered by the men and women who lead organizations: *unlearning*.

One of the first references to the idea of organizational unlearning was in an article by Bo Hedberg in 1981. According to Hedberg, "Knowledge grows, and simultaneously it becomes obsolete as reality changes. Understanding involves both learning new knowledge and discarding obsolete and misleading knowledge."[17]

In other words, gaining new knowledge first requires unlearning knowledge that is no longer of use or that has become outdated and an obstacle in the way of our forward progress. It's this unlearning that often goes missing in leaders and the organizations they lead. You only have to look at the changing of the S&P 500 guard since 1990 to find evidence of who listened and applied both lessons and who did not. The people leading the companies that are winning today—Apple, Amazon, Google, and other tech firms—took these lessons to heart, while the losers, including Sears, Lehman Brothers, and General Electric (the last remaining original member of the S&P 500, which departed the list on

June 26, 2018, having topped the list as recently as 2005, and until 2013 was still in the top five) did not.

Disruption does not actually apply to organizations. The truth is it applies to *individuals*. Consider what great leaders and the great companies they lead have in common. They have cultivated a capability within themselves to innovate, adapt, and anticipate the future. They invest in experiences that enable them to grow; they seek situations that are uncomfortable, uncertain, and the results unknown. They create mechanisms to experiment quickly, and safely gather new information to evolve into something better. They succeed over the long term by not holding on to what once brought them success. How they succeed isn't magical; it's methodical. It's not down to serendipity or luck—they have intentional systems.

In my own experience working all around the world with executives and teams—from disruptive start-ups to the globally renowned behemoths of the Fortune 500—I've seen firsthand the struggle both great and growing leaders face as they seek to lead innovation in their markets. It prompted me to coauthor my first book, the international bestseller *Lean Enterprise: How High Performance Organizations Innovate at Scale*, for the Eric Ries Lean Series. It gave me the opportunity to interview, work with, advise, and coach hundreds of business and technology leaders and to research thousands of companies and case studies to discover what leads to higher performance and outstanding accomplishments.

I've seen what enables certain leaders to accelerate and what makes others stop in their tracks. In times past, an individual's knowledge would last a lifetime. Indeed, knowledge would be passed down for many generations and still be highly useful. Yet, as the pace of innovation increases, once-useful knowledge now becomes rapidly obsolete—hence the need to consider a system of unlearning. Exceptional leaders have discovered it's not how smart they are, how much they know, how long they've been in an industry, or what they have learned. It's the ability to recognize when to unlearn and when to let go of past success and their outdated thinking and behaviors, and innovate new mindsets and methods to achieve extraordinary results.

Yes, learning is one part, but the answer is not only to learn. We struggle even more to know what to let go of, move away from, and *unlearn.*

In the next chapter, we'll consider exactly *how* you can leverage the power of unlearning to your own advantage—and that of your teams and organizations.

2

How to Unlearn

When we really delve into the reasons for why we can't let something go,
there are only two: an attachment to the past or a fear for the future.
—Marie Kondō

ost leaders today know they must constantly transform the way
they do business—making decisions much more quickly, responding to fast-changing markets with greater agility, better addressing
customer needs, and more. One of the great problems with moving away
from old ways of doing business to new is that the neural pathways of the
men and women who lead these organizations have become fixed and
rigid over time. Leaders get caught in a myopic view of the world around
them, mainly informed and biased by their daily field of operations.

The push for immediate results, coupled with overloaded schedules
and pressure to execute decisions and deliver faster, provide them with
few opportunities to reflect on results. Plans get interrupted by problems, and context switching becomes an uncontrolled hidden cost. Many
leaders never have the time to just *think*—to deeply consider problems
and potential alternative options. As a result, they implement tactical,
point solutions that optimize short-term business efficiency and revenue
capture, but ultimately lose sight of the bigger vision, challenges, and
experiences for their customers. They fail to learn—or more important,

unlearn—the behaviors and mindsets that are limiting their effectiveness and trapping them and their business in a cycle that has little left to give. All too often this motion is mistaken for progress.

Believe me, it's not.

When leaders do find a moment to take time out, attend the occasional innovation off-site, weekend retreat, or week-long program at a prestigious, internationally renowned university, business school, or association, they return to the workplace brimming with new ideas and initiatives. But in most cases, they quickly revert to their previous conditioned and comfortable patterns of behavior and thinking, further crushed by the reality they face upon their return.

It should be no surprise, therefore, that most training and development efforts in businesses today routinely fail to hit the mark. A recent *Harvard Business Review* article points out that American businesses spend a tremendous amount of money on employee training and education. In 2015, this number was estimated to be approximately $160 billion in the United States, and $356 billion globally. Yet only one in four attendees say the training was critical to business outcomes and "For the most part, the learning doesn't lead to better organizational performance, because people soon revert to their old ways of doing things."[1]

Unlearning is different. It isn't a one-and-done event—it's a *system*: a system of letting go and adapting to the situational reality of the present as we look to the future. It's recognizing that whatever it is that we have previously done may no longer be useful at this moment. Your mission is to develop the capability to know when to move away from outdated information, take in new information to inform your thinking, and adapt your behaviors as a result.

Courage is the recognition that what you are doing is not working for you, letting go, and taking action to do what is needed to progress. The first breakthrough is the realization that you must, in fact, *unlearn*. By identifying the aspiration or outcome you wish to achieve—paired with the deliberate practice to get there—you can start to move toward your desired state and achieve extraordinary results.

The Cycle of Unlearning

The system of unlearning is based on a three-step approach to individual and collective growth that I have dubbed the Cycle of Unlearning (Figure 2.1). I have developed this system over years of working with, advising, and coaching outstanding executives, employees, and teams. I will show you how high performers use this system naturally, even unintentionally, and tell you how you can harness it into a conscious act of cultivating your character and capabilities for growth and impact.

Adopting the Cycle of Unlearning doesn't rely on being smart, or lucky, or desperate, or all of the above. It relies only on *you*—your courage and commitment to use it intentionally in your work and your life to achieve extraordinary results.

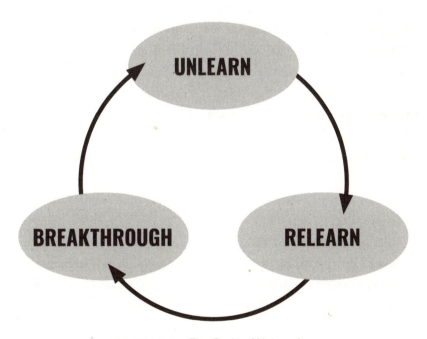

FIGURE 2.1.   The Cycle of Unlearning

Step One: Unlearn

There are a variety of reasons why individuals get stuck doing the same things over and over again, instead of leading innovation in their markets. The main one is the erroneous belief that doing what brought you success today will bring you success tomorrow. Unfortunately, the systems, models, and methods that work today can actually *limit* your ability to change—and succeed—tomorrow.

The core premise of this book assumes you possess an eager desire to learn, and a willingness to unlearn, when you recognize once-useful mindsets and behaviors are now limiting your current and future success. Are you as an individual open to the idea that what you're doing might not be optimal, but instead outdated or obsolete? This is the self-awareness, the humility, the curiosity required to seek growth. And this is why we must make space and time for new information to come in.

Do you have the courage to recognize that what you are doing is not working, be willing to accept it, let go, and try something different? What aspirations do you have but yet feel unclear about where to start? Have you set expectations of yourself but not delivered your desired outcome, citing excuses or hardships you know you're unwilling to face? What challenge are you struggling with, and you've tried all your tools yet still seem stuck? These are clear signals you are limiting your performance or have hit a local maximum, and that it's time to begin the Cycle of Unlearning.

Unlearning does not lead with words; it leads with action. You can't just say, "Yeah, of course I want to unlearn." You must first embrace your purpose by clarifying your *why* and your *what*. Why exactly do you want to unlearn? What specifically do you want to unlearn?

Do you believe this is important? Are you open to it? Are you curious? Do you agree there could be a better answer other than your own, an alternative way to achieve better results? When you can answer "yes" to these questions, then it's time to focus on the specifics of what you want to unlearn.

This first step in the Cycle of Unlearning requires courage, self-awareness, and humility to accept that your own beliefs, mindsets, or behaviors are limiting your potential and current performance and that you must consciously move away from them. This allows you to be open to new approaches and get unstuck. The key to unlocking the capability to continuously adapt and affect your environment and personal development starts with *you*. By identifying the aspiration or outcome you wish to achieve—quantifying and holding yourself accountable for it—you can start to move toward your desired state and achieve extraordinary results.

As Einstein famously said, "We cannot resolve a problem by using the same thinking that created it." The same is true as we unlearn. It's only through courage, curiosity, and identifying what we desire to unlearn that we can take the next step: to relearn.

Step Two: Relearn

As you unlearn your current limiting but ingrained methods, behaviors, and thinking, you can take in new data, information, and perspectives. And by considering all this new input, you naturally challenge your existing mental models of the world. It is by leveraging these insights that you can seek improvement, adaptation, and growth. By exploring difficult tasks, you will discover a tremendous amount about yourself. You'll understand your mind and body's natural resistance, as well as the discipline and power of deliberate practice to overcome internal and external obstacles to succeed. You'll build your own personal resilience and self-belief.

But there are immense challenges to relearning effectively, and we create many of these challenges ourselves. First, you must be willing to adapt and be open to information that goes against your inherent beliefs—that may be at odds with what you have always been told or taught to do. Second, you may need to learn how to learn again. Finally, you must create an environment for relearning to happen in a meaningful, yet often challenging, space outside your existing comfort zone.

The first step in the Cycle of Unlearning demonstrates you recognize the need to innovate. However, it's in this second step that you build confidence, capability, and momentum. You're relearning—deliberately.

What you're trying to do is get better information and learn to see, sense, and listen differently, to respond and act differently. Relearning is the space where you can experiment—where you can get to grips with uncertainty—through deliberate, practical, and experiential learning.

The prerequisite to relearning is questioning your current beliefs for what you consider to be possible. You must think big and challenge your assumptions of the world. But while you think big, you must also start small. It's creating the bounded context of relearning—small steps and experiments that create the safe-to-fail environment required to break through.

I demonstrate in examples, client stories, and case studies referenced throughout this book that *safety*—be it psychological, physical, or economic—has been proven to be a leading indicator for higher performance and extraordinary results.[2] Especially psychological safety, defined by Boston University's William A. Khan as "being able to show and employ one's self without fear of negative consequences of self-image, status, or career." Creating a space to allow experimentation to happen in a controlled and recoverable manner, with safe-to-fail experiments and a high level of psychological safety, enables people to make adjustments to their existing behaviors, explore the edges of their universe, and start to grow.

That's the reason we think big but start small—so we're not taking unrecoverable risks. You're operating outside your comfort zone, but neither you nor your organization or team will trigger catastrophic consequences if it doesn't work out as predicted. In fact, you should not expect it to as you take your first steps into the unknown. I will show you how to create a safe environment and design safe-to-fail experiments as you relearn what is necessary to achieve the final step of the transformation: breakthrough.

Step Three: Breakthrough

Once you—whatever your position, from the C-suite to the shop floor—learn how to relearn and open yourself up to new information flows, networks, and systems from every possible source, you are poised to develop the kind of breakthrough thinking that has the potential to vault you into the lead. Breakthrough is the result of unlearning and then relearning—it's the new information and insights that come out of the first two steps of the Cycle of Unlearning. The information and insights are extremely powerful because they inform and guide your behaviors, perspective, and mindset.

I cannot count the number of times I've interviewed executives and leaders in organizations whose first comment is, "What we really need is to change the mindset here." Leaders believe they simply need to tell people to *think* differently, and they will *act* differently. This is a fallacy that must, in fact, be unlearned. The way to think differently is to act differently. When you act differently, you start to see and experience the world differently, impacting your mindset as a result. And because you're realizing the benefits of adapting your behaviors and gaining new perspectives that impact your mindset, you become open to unlearning your behaviors more often. It's an accelerant.

As we break free of our existing mental models and methods, we learn to let go of the past to achieve extraordinary results. We realize that as the world is constantly evolving, innovating, and progressing, so too must we. Persisting with the same thinking and behaviors inhibits ongoing and future success. Our breakthroughs provide an opportunity to reflect on the lessons we have learned from relearning and provide a springboard for tackling bigger and more audacious challenges.

This process can be as simple as asking yourself what went well, not so well, and what you would do differently if you were to try and unlearn the same challenge again. Using this information and insight and feeding it forward to future loops of the Cycle of Unlearning means every loop of the cycle results in deeper insight, greater impact, and growth.

After breakthrough, the cycle starts all over again as leaders push forward with new innovations, new ideas, and new ways of doing business. The constant danger, however, is that complacency may set in and the commitment to keep pushing forward may waver. Slowly but surely, we can start to settle—slipping back into our old habits, instead of amplifying the virtuous cycle toward further success.

Unlearning is not an event. It is ongoing and continuous—a habit and deliberate practice in itself. By breaking through, what we're really trying to achieve is: (1) reflect on our results; (2) make our course corrections; and (3) use the new information and momentum to keep accelerating through the loop again, leading to new breakthroughs.

What you put into the Cycle of Unlearning is up to you and depends on your personal aspirations and outcomes for growth. The remarkable power of this system is revealed when you start with one small challenge you face or aspiration you want to achieve, and then think about how you can apply it to ever larger and more complex challenges or aspirations until finally—*everything*.

You can use this system to solve all sorts of problems and challenges or leverage any kind of opportunity. In doing so, you'll learn how to make better decisions when you're faced with difficult circumstances and uncertain situations. People often think the only way to achieve big results is to start big, go big, bet big. This is not true. Instead, think big but start small. Try many alternatives. You can make lots of small bets—not just one big bet—to find the breakthrough that is most impactful for you.

Failure is to do nothing. It's to not act. To do *anything* means it will result in some new, even surprising information or insight; so, no matter what, it's always a positive result for *you*. You're always going to learn something, discover something, or invalidate something.

As philosopher Eric Hoffer said, "In a time of drastic change it is the learners who inherit the future. The learned usually find themselves equipped to live in a world that no longer exists."

UNLEARNING PROMPTS

- Where are you falling short of your expectations?
- Where are you not seeing the outcomes you want?
- What are you willing to do to affect those outcomes?
- How could you get out of your comfort zone and succeed?
- What would thinking BIG but starting small be for you?

Once you've answered these questions, then you are ready to commence your Cycle of Unlearning to achieve extraordinary results, impact, and growth.

Unlearning in Action

International Airlines Group (IAG)—the parent company of Aer Lingus, British Airways, Iberia, LEVEL, Vueling, Avios Group Limited, and IAG Cargo—is the third largest airline group in Europe and the sixth largest in the world, based on revenue of €22.9 billion in 2017. It has more than 63,000 employees, 547 aircraft, and carries some 105 million passengers each year.[3] A few years ago, the company came to the realization that sending its executives and senior managers to short training workshops or classes was not enough to move the needle sufficiently to disrupt their behaviors and mindsets. They rightly believed that bringing about real transformation would require the much deeper and longer commitment of its most experienced leaders.

IAG asked, "How can we think big and start small to have a systemic and sustained impact on how our leaders lead and on how we lead our industry?"

Their answer? What if six of IAG's most senior leaders were taken out of cross-company business divisions for *eight weeks*—completely removed from their day-to-day responsibilities—with the mission to launch new businesses to disrupt their existing business and, in turn, themselves. Could this initiative challenge the senior leaders' thinking and create new neural pathways, new habits, and new ways to innovate and work by giving them the time and focus to embrace the reality of their industry's commoditization, and the uncertainty of how to respond to it?

As Anders Ericsson—expert on performance and author of *Peak: Secrets from the New Science of Expertise*—suggests, this sort of deliberate practice with executives and business leaders, given the mission to radically reinvent their business, ways of working, and themselves, could make a tremendous difference in the organization's outcomes. By taking on challenges outside their comfort zones and by experimenting with new methods, tools, and techniques, these leaders could break free of fixed behaviors and myopic mindsets, and catapult to higher levels of performance.

IAG realized that they couldn't keep doing the same one-day innovation off-sites that delivered *too little*, or wait on multiyear transformational programs that arrived *too late*. They needed to create a sustainable system to drive innovation in their company, and stop doing the same old actions and expecting different results. So IAG designed a purpose-built petri dish to *unlearn* the way these leaders would do innovation, *relearn* by running six of their most senior people through an eight-week "Catapult," and get the breakthroughs they desired as a result of working, experiencing, and seeing the world in a different way.

I had the opportunity to work with this team from IAG as we tackled the Catapult challenge. The team's mission was to disrupt themselves and their existing business by working through lots of different ideas, and then testing them to figure out which ones would work and which ones wouldn't. We would move people outside their comfort zones and remove them from their day-to-day contexts so they would have a safe environment to be more expansive, unlearn old ways of working, relearn new ways of working, and develop the breakthrough thinking and behavior that would fuel individual growth and systemic impact.

They would learn by doing—with time, focus, and permission to be bold. Failure was to do what had been done before, and to not achieve the outcome we set: to discover six ideas that had the potential to change the course of their industry, and in turn transform IAG and themselves.

Early in the eight-week Catapult immersion, one of the participating IAG team members came up with an idea they believed would revolutionize the experience for how people would book travel. The airline industry is uniquely complex when it comes to reserving and buying tickets because there are so many different ways to do so. You can book it directly with the airline, with a travel agent, with a flight aggregator, or even at the airport on your travel day. The way you book a flight determines how much the airline actually knows about you and what kind of service it can provide.

If you are a loyal, premium flyer, airlines want to reward your behavior by making you feel special—perhaps the gate agent upgrades you to first class. However, if you booked your ticket through a travel agent or intermediator, the airline may not have your membership information attached to your ticket. So when you walk up to the counter, the agent may not have the information on hand that highlights your premium status, and therefore may not give you the special treatment you are used to.

This is an unsatisfying experience for any airline's customers, and one the airlines aspire to resolve. They want to make you feel special by providing a contextual offer or personalized experience based on who you are, the situation you're in, and the data you believe they should know about you but can't.

What's ironic about this situation is, of all industries, airlines actually have the most information about their customers. They know your name, your address, how much you fly, where you fly from, and where you fly to. They know what you like to eat and drink, what you buy from their in-flight duty-free stores, and whether you prefer luxury or economy. They know if you use their affiliated hotels, rental car agencies, and other third-party offerings. They know if you're a trusted traveler, or if you deserve extra scrutiny by airport security. In the airline industry, the company with the biggest, most expansive platform and network wins.

So when a team member in the Catapult took a look at this system with a view to improving it, he displayed all the signs of the typical classroom-taught, corporate-conditioned approach to innovation. He was an expert, so not only did he believe he had all the answers, he was convinced his great first idea was the *best* idea: a new booking platform. He was certain this idea was going to be loved by customers and transform the business—and the industry—if everyone just got on board with it. He defaulted to High-Paid Person's Opinion (HiPPO) mode, pushing his ideas on people instead of pulling ideas from the company's customers.

What was truly needed was for this Catapult team member to unlearn all his classically conditioned thinking and behaviors around product innovation.

We encouraged him to sketch a simple prototype of this new booking platform and test it on some real, live customers. The feedback from the testing was not good. In fact, it was dreadful. Customers didn't like it—at all.

He rejected this feedback, thinking that the polling must have been faulty and we were testing with the wrong customer base. "Customers who really understood airline pricing and ticket types would understand why it was such a great new product—get me the right customers for this idea," he said. So we repeated the process. Again, we got the same result and the same response. He was convinced that the customers didn't understand what we were offering them, and so we repeated the process again, and again. After about four cycles—with the same undesired result—I sat down with him to reflect.

"What do you think the issue is?" I asked.

"It's the *idea*, not the *customer*," he said.

This leader entered the Cycle of Unlearning without realizing it. Upon iteration, reflection, and retrospection, the breakthrough came. *Our* mindset and behavior is the problem, not our *customers'*. By embracing the Cycle of Unlearning his thinking flipped 180 degrees. He grasped the benefit of the new behavior and started to accelerate his unlearning of old thinking and behaviors.

This leader came to the realization that every "great" idea, every new innovation, is at best a guess—a belief and hypothesis—and we must design experiments to test the assumptions of our hypothesis, ideally with the customers we are designing for. Their feedback is the most authoritative and objective guide through the uncertainty inherent in innovation. When we start to see the world this way, everything becomes an opportunity to unlearn, relearn, and break through. This IAG leader ended up becoming one of the standout members of the team, because he started to embrace the Cycle of Unlearning in every aspect of his work. He shifted his behavior to unlearn and relearn everything he thought he knew. He became curious again and was able to escape the "I (must) know all the answers" trap by turning obstacles to unlearning into opportunities for impact.

He had moved from a *know* it all to an _unlearn_ it all.

IAG realized that the Catapult was just the start—the first small step. By setting an aspiration to discover six ideas to change the course of their industry and transform the company and its leadership, IAG identified numerous industry innovations. They started their own venture fund, the Hanger 51 accelerator program—a collaboration with industry start-ups and disruptors—to further challenge their thinking and behaviors, leveraging and innovating their existing assets. They adopted blockchain technology to build the first digital identity service to help airlines share data safely and securely when passengers take connecting flights. They created simple ways for customers to record and share trips, making sure that the customers never forget their experiences and adventures. And they leveraged predictive analytics to analyze unstructured customer feedback by focusing on automatically categorizing the data and visualizing key insights in just minutes (what had normally taken months of manual data analysis), thereby improving their services in context for customers.[4]

Most recently, IAG demonstrated that while they started small, they are still thinking BIG. In March 2017, IAG launched an entirely new transatlantic airline, LEVEL, in response to increased competition in the low-cost, long-haul market. LEVEL sold 52,000 seats within two days of being established, and more than 147,000 seats after little more than a month and a half, far exceeding IAG's expectations.[5]

While all these innovations were outstanding breakthroughs for IAG in their industry, the biggest impact has been much more lasting, profound, and systemic—the change in leadership *mindset*. Leaders throughout the organization, inspired by the Catapult experience, went back to the company with newly found confidence and capability to get uncomfortable and unlearn, while helping others to unlearn, relearn, and break through.

Stephen Scott, chief digital officer for IAG's Avios Group Limited, shared a key reflection from the experience: "Part of unlearning is not getting stuck doing only what worked in the past. When 97 percent of people think you should just go back to doing what you've been doing, or resist the change you are trying to make, you know you're on to something, and that's where the breakthrough journey begins . . ." The company and its leadership now see uncertainty as an opportunity to get outside their comfort zone, challenge themselves, and win.

When We Should Apply the Cycle of Unlearning

Now that we have a better understanding of how the Cycle of Unlearning works, this begs the question: *When* should we unlearn? You might not be surprised to discover that my answer to that question is, "Always," but let's first consider some of the kinds of signals that should tell you it's time to take an immediate loop through the Cycle of Unlearning.

One compelling situation is when you have tried everything to resolve a challenge, but you haven't achieved the aspiration or outcome you desire, you haven't lived up to your expectations, or you're simply stuck. Just as IAG leadership realized innovation off-sites or classroom certifications weren't going to provide a lasting impact on their executives' long-term behaviors or mindsets, you too must be courageous enough to recognize what you're doing isn't working, and commit to taking an alternative, potentially *radical*, approach.

Another situation is when new information triggers new understanding of the world, such as the insights Patrick Mouratoglou first shared with Serena Williams. With technology advancing at near-exponential rates and business markets changing almost as quickly, we are constantly bombarded with new information. If we take time to absorb this information—an idea sparked by a chance conversation, insight gained by dealing with a customer, or a game-changing new technology—we can turn to the Cycle of Unlearning to help us embrace new approaches that will bring us success in the future.

While these situations are pivotal moments to unlearn, the ideal state is not to be in a situation triggered by existential threats or crises, and—as I suggested at the beginning of this book—to instead adopt the practice of unlearning regularly, habitually, as we do breathing and living itself.

With ongoing, deliberate practice, each one of us has the ability to leverage unlearning instinctively and use it intentionally, not only as a response when there is no option. We can then develop a capability to solve any challenge we face or aspiration we wish to achieve simply by unlearning what is holding us back, relearning new behaviors to address it, and breaking through to leap ahead. This unique capability is what enables leaders to continually find new and higher levels of performance, often beyond what they thought they, their teams, and their businesses were initially capable of.

The single most important action of any leader is to model the behaviors you wish to see others exhibit in the organization. By cultivating the practice of unlearning your own mindset and behaviors you will begin to make unlearning a part of your organization's culture—encouraging others to unlearn and feel safe to do so. The way you behave reflects the values and expectations you have of yourself and of others.

But, in some ways, our minds conspire against us. We are physically and psychologically hardwired to respond to our environments—and to the information we receive from a variety of sources—in certain premeditated and programmed ways. Understanding how this affects our decision making, and how we must adapt to address it, is critically important to being able to succeed in adopting the Cycle of Unlearning.

3

Unlearning the Obstacles to Unlearning

The greater the obstacle, the more glory in overcoming it.
—Molière

nlearning requires courage, curiosity, and being comfortable with getting uncomfortable. To achieve the aspirations and outcomes we desire, we must let go of unworkable values, assumptions, and beliefs that block or inhibit our future development. We have to be open to accept that our existing conditioning may be limiting our future success.

Often the most challenging obstacle to unlearning is ourselves: our old thought patterns that make us blind to new possibilities and new ways of improving. Obstacles may be internal, external, or contextual, but whatever their origin, they conspire to keep us firmly stuck in the status quo. They include:

- **Our leadership conditioning:** How we've been taught to lead and the underlying assumptions of leadership we carry within us are based on our experience of the world. Our own definition of leadership success is most influenced by what we observe in our daily work, from the leaders we follow and the organizations in which we work—the majority of which are still anchored in practices and principles established during the nineteenth-century Industrial Revolution.

- **Our knowledge threshold:** Our current understanding of how the world works is based on the information we have available and consider true and correct. As children, we begin as empty vessels that absorb new experiences that shape our understanding, making one mental leap after another, each opening up a new and previously inaccessible way of thinking. But we fill up with expertise, or give up on what's too challenging. Our beginner's mind is forgotten, and so, too, our quest to continue to explore.

- **Our biases:** The psychologically and neurologically preprogrammed ways we attempt to simplify the complexity of the world, often based on poor information and inadequate situational awareness. We hurry decisions, apply quick fixes and Band-Aids, and speed up without ever slowing down to reflect and consider what is really in front of us. We rarely give ourselves the time and the space to pause, process, and then persevere with the promise that the results will be better in the end.

- **Our desire to always be correct:** The force of our ego and its powerful influence over us. Ego is often the enemy of self-awareness, and it is the trigger for situations of high stress, fear, and distrust. To be smart is to demonstrate your breadth of knowledge and know-how—the majority of organizations promote on that basis—hence the risk of embarrassment at being wrong raises barriers preventing us from engaging in anything inherently uncertain or unknown (where growth happens).

- **Our focus on reward and recognition:** Praise from an early age, knowing the correct answer in class, corporate structures that reward the status quo and those who behave and do as they are told. We create contingent relationships and tell humans if they *do this,* they will *get that.* Once framed this way, we naturally only focus on the *get that* side of the equation. We miss the purpose of *do this* and forget the inherent value of why we might do it in the first place. No better is this exemplified than by the unintended consequences and negative behaviors driven by the *get that* rewards of big bonuses for individuals that drove the behavior that contributed toward the global financial crisis.

- **Our ability (or inability) to deal with uncertainty and risk:** The extent to which we try to find certainty and avoid risk in the world around us. Researchers have found that humans naturally prefer both predictable positive *and* negative consequences over uncertainty.[6] A team led by Archy de Berke found that when the odds approach 50:50 and uncertainty is at its peak, then dopamine in our brain surges and the sympathetic nervous system is triggered— preparing the body to take dramatic action. Stress increases, and the mind therefore resists options that are uncertain. Translating this into a business context, we do everything we can as leaders to avoid uncertain outcomes.

- **Our curiosity (or lack thereof):** The extent to which we are fascinated by new information and unanswered questions, and are motivated to seek it in all we do and to discover even more. Curiosity is what drives us to step out of the status quo of our day-to-day existence, pushing the boundaries of what we know. For instance, when was the last time someone presented you with an idea at odds with your viewpoint, and you responded with, "Interesting, tell me more," instead of immediately rejecting it?

- **Our environment:** The context, structure, and social norms of our workplace, the industries and markets in which we do business, the communities in which we live, and the world as a whole. What our environment values, we value. Does yours value unlearning, and actively practice it as the Romans once did?

Unlearning is an act of vulnerability—of leaving behind the certainty of what you know and opening yourself up to uncertainty. It is an acknowledgment that what you know is not sufficient and that new information, new thinking, and new behaviors are necessary to help you grow and have impact.

The Success Trap

For most people, normalizing vulnerability—let alone failure—goes against all their leadership conditioning. Prevailing definitions of success set forth the idea that you'll achieve what you want through hard work, always knowing the correct answer, and getting it right the first time.

Similarly, the way we view success can be an obstacle in itself because success can limit our willingness and curiosity to unlearn. When people have a history of positive results, they become wedded to the behaviors they attribute to the rewards and recognition related to those results. These positive results make individuals reticent to try different approaches because they don't want to fail; they fear experiencing any type of negative result. The more successful people are, the more fearful they become to try untested methods or alternative techniques because they're afraid their stellar record, prestige, or personal brand will be destroyed.

Many executive teams have built their careers on methodologies and mindsets that are no longer valid, and they grow frustrated with teams that wish to embrace a more experimental, evidence-based approach of working—an approach which is unknown to them, but more important, the perceived results uncertain.

For example, when recruited to a new company, the majority of CEOs and executives immediately push the organization—and the people within it—to adapt to their own preferred leadership style and systems, regardless of what the business actually needs. They tell themselves that everything is great because they design systems that work for *them*, not the people who have to work *within* that system. They ask for reports that are consistent across the entire organization because it's easy for *them* to compare many initiatives, and it's a system that's known and comfortable for them to command and control. This is a mistake and must be unlearned. Instead they should be curious to understand what is important for a given initiative, and then design custom controls for each initiative based on the problem it's trying to solve.

Copy-and-paste organizational redesigns and methodology rollouts create activity, much output, and are claimed to be successful. Yet, few deliver the desired outcomes, and the leaders who employ them rarely measure and hold themselves accountable to these outcomes before moving to the next role. They rinse, repeat, and then disappear before the consequences of their actions come to fruition.

This problem and perspective is so elegantly captured by T. S. Eliot: "Nothing pleases people more than to go on thinking what they have always thought, and at the same time imagine that they are thinking something new and daring: It combines the advantage of security with the delight of adventure."

This is status-quo leadership: applying the same models and methods everywhere you go. And while a particular approach may have once worked for you, chances are it's no longer valid. It should therefore be no surprise that 84 percent of business transformations fail, primarily attributed to leadership not being prepared to change their own behavior.[1]

Success can reinforce and strengthen attribution biases, such as blaming luck, chance, or external factors when you don't get your desired result, and taking credit for success when you do. Bill Gates famously said, "Success is a lousy teacher. It seduces smart people into thinking they can't lose." Marshall Goldsmith echoed this in the title of his book *What Got You Here Won't Get You There*. What made you successful in the past might not make you successful at the next thing—or the next.

Nothing that's worthwhile is ever easy, yet few people are willing to invest the effort or take the time required to develop the mastery to unlearn and relearn. We seek shortcuts, quick tips, or just enough education to perform before switching our time and thoughts to the next trending tactic, never really developing much beyond shallow knowledge and novice know-how. Says Anders Ericsson, "This is a fundamental truth about any sort of practice: If you never push yourself beyond your comfort zone, you will never improve."

The Obstacles We Create

Another trap our brain sets to stick to the status quo rather than trying something new is our intense desire to be correct. Kids are constantly adjusting, figuring, and evolving. Our development is based on trial and error, experience, and discovery. This all begins to change, however, when we are enrolled in the school system. We train our children *what* to think, not *how* to think, and further propagate this conformity throughout higher education and into professional and corporate careers.

In the most popular TED talk of all time, "Do schools kill creativity?," Sir Ken Robinson explains how the school system creates fear of having the wrong answer in children. Says Robinson:

> . . . kids will take a chance. If they don't know, they'll have a go. Am I right? They're not frightened of being wrong. I don't mean to say that being wrong is the same thing as being creative. What we do know is, if you're not prepared to be wrong, you'll never come up with anything original . . . And by the time they get to be adults, most kids have lost that capacity. They have become frightened of being wrong. And we run our companies like this. We stigmatize mistakes. And we're now running national education systems where mistakes are the worst thing you can make. And the result is that we are educating people out of their creative capacities.[2]

Trying to lay blame solely on the education system is unfair, as this thinking and behavior is reinforced and refined as we progress through the corporate structures and cultures in which we reside, where making mistakes is not only *not* tolerated by managers, but their sole function is to eradicate all potential for them to occur, along with the people who might make them. We are a product of our environment, the people we surround ourselves with, and the company we work within. How does your environment value taking a chance, to be wrong, or to make mistakes?

Ron Westrum, a professor of sociology at Eastern Michigan University, developed the Three Cultures Model to explain how organizations process information (Table 3.1).[3] According to Westrum, the three cultures are:

PATHOLOGICAL	BUREAUCRATIC	GENERATIVE
Power-oriented culture marked by:	Rule-oriented culture marked by:	Performance-oriented culture marked by:
Low cooperation	Modest cooperation	High cooperation
Messengers shot	Messengers neglected	Messengers trained
Responsibilities shirked	Narrow responsibilities	Risks shared
Bridging discouraged	Bridging tolerated	Bridging encouraged
Failure leads to scapegoating	Failure leads to justice	Failure leads to inquiry
Novelty crushed	Novelty leads to problems	Novelty implemented

TABLE 3.1. Three Cultures Model

These are very different environments, and they result in very different behaviors and mindsets. In my experience, the cultures in the vast majority of organizations today are either of the pathological or the bureaucratic type anchored in the Industrial Era. This explains why experimenting with learning new skills and capabilities, let alone unlearning limiting conditioned behaviors, is so difficult. Managers within pathological and bureaucratic environments stick to the comfort of how "we've always done it around here," ingenuity becomes suppressed and avoided at all costs, and employees keep their heads down, punch the clock, and collect their paychecks.

What separates truly great environments from the rest of the pack is a generative, performance-oriented culture where cooperation is high and there's a comfort with discomfort. People aren't afraid to try new things: They can take a chance, be wrong, and use the information they discover to improve themselves, their work, and the companies for which they work. They have a sense of safety with encouragement, freedom with accountability, and ownership for their actions—all of which lead to better outcomes. I'll show you how Capital One, NASA, the NHS, and others have created this kind of culture, and the steps they took to unlearn and leap ahead, empowering their people to extraordinary results.

UNLEARNING PROMPTS

Pause for a moment and reflect on Westrum's Three Cultures Model:

- In which culture would you position yourself, your team, and your organization against each behavior?
- Where are you not living up to the expectations you and your team have set for yourselves as to how you wish to behave?
- Which one characteristic is holding you back the most?
- For that one characteristic, where do you aspire to be?
- What small step could you take to get there, and be better?

Moving from one culture to another will require unlearning and relearning, but by focusing on one aspect at a time, with deliberate practice it is possible to get there.

Turning Obstacles into Opportunity

As I mentioned earlier, it's far better to adopt the Cycle of Unlearning *before* you and your organization are in crisis than *after*. But, of course, many leaders and organizations do find themselves in crisis, and they wonder what they can do to get out of it.

One of my favorite existential threat stories is when Andy Grove was at the helm of Intel, and he realized that the business they were in at the time—memory chips, which were becoming commodities—was going to die. Grove recognized that Intel was experiencing an existential threat, and he pivoted the company to the production of microprocessors, a category that Intel stole from its Japanese competitors (which had 60 percent market share) and eventually came to dominate.

Said Grove about the decision:

> I looked out the window at the Ferris wheel of the Great America amusement park revolving in the distance, then I turned back to Gordon and I asked, "If we got kicked out and the board brought in a new CEO, what do you think he would do?" Gordon answered without hesitation, "He would get us out of memories." I stared at him, numb, then said, "Why shouldn't you and I walk out the door, come back in, and do it ourselves?"[4]

And that's exactly what they did. The best leaders don't have all the answers; they ask better questions. The result of better questions—or as I call them, unlearning prompts—is better answers.

Andy Grove called these events that change the way we think or act *strategic inflection points*, and he explained that they could arise due to a variety of reasons, including new technologies, changes in the regulatory environment, or a shift in customer values or preferences. In his book *Only the Paranoid Survive*, Grove provided the following definition of the term:

A strategic inflection point is a time in the life of a business when its fundamentals are about to change. That change can mean an opportunity to rise to new heights. But it may just as likely signal the beginning of the end.

The idea of strategic inflection points applies not only to organizations but to individuals, too. People face defining moments during their lives that require unknown or unfamiliar abilities to pass through. The key to succeed is to have courage, humility, and a system to recognize these inflection points, take action, and unlearn.

As the rate of innovation increases, so too will the frequency that inflection points occur. The question is not if you'll be impacted by one, but when. The options are therefore to hope it doesn't happen to you, to wait for it to happen (meaning you're often too late or ill equipped to respond), or to own and create them for yourself by mastering a system to intentionally unlearn, discover new information, and prompt new thinking and behaviors to progress and grow.

There are an infinite number of ways we can shake up our perspectives and break out of our ruts. Together with artist Peter Schmidt, musician and producer Brian Eno created a deck of cards printed with more than 100 oblique strategies they developed to break deadlocks in creative situations. These strategies help artists to reframe their thinking or behavior, and include prompts such as:

- Discover the recipes you are using and abandon them.
- What wouldn't you do?
- Honor thy error as a hidden intention.
- Always first steps.
- Toward the insignificant.
- Make a list of everything you might do and do the last thing on the list.
- Take away the elements in order of apparent non-importance.

When faced with a difficult dilemma, the idea is to draw a card, follow the recommended strategy, and enjoy the benefits of the resulting lateral thinking and action. Intentional intervention can be the key to discovering new information and new insights, and having breakthroughs as a result.

Putting the Magic Back into Disney's Magic Kingdom

Disneyland—the 1950s-vintage creation of filmmaker Walt Disney and his brother Roy—bills itself as "the Happiest Place on Earth." And for generations of visitors to Southern California's Disneyland and to its much-larger corporate sibling, Walt Disney World in Orlando, Florida, these theme parks are both centerpiece and home to Disney's very special brand of magic.

However, in the mid-2000s—much like the toxic stew slowly bubbling in the Wicked Witch's black cauldron in Snow White's Scary Adventures ride—there was big trouble brewing in this happiest of places. Customers were voting with their feet, with crucial metrics such as guest "intent to return" falling precipitously. Approximately one-half of first-time guests reported that they would not be returning to Walt Disney World, an alarming statistic for Disney executives. Why was it so difficult for the very smart people who ran Disney's theme parks (which accounted for $18.4 billion of the company's overall 2017 revenues of $55.1 billion)[5] to bring back the magic that so many devoted fans fondly remember from their youth?

In 2008, Disney's executive team decided it was time to take bold action to reverse the parks' downward slide. Parks division top executives Jay Rasulo and Al Weiss and then-president of Walt Disney World, Meg Crofton, chartered a team to explore how "to reinvent the vacation experience—and keep [Disney World] relevant." They formed a small, cross-functional team dubbed the "Founding Five." The team was comprised of SVP of technology Andy Schwalb, parks VP Jim MacPhee, business development VP John Padgett, and two executives from the fabled Imagineering department, Kevin Rice and Eric Jacobson.

Their mission? To rekindle the Disney magic and the mindset of its leaders.

Like IAG, they would need to unlearn much of what they had always done and relearn a new way to discover the illusive breakthroughs both they and their business craved.

Initially, the Founding Five struggled—coming up with the Band-Aid solutions to age-old problems using the same old ways of thinking to fix the problems right in front of their noses. Even the best business leaders can suffer from a myopic view of the world around them that is mainly informed and biased by their daily field of operations. The team was well aware of the park's problems—the crowds, the long lines, the endless hops back and forth across the park as guests tried to maximize their experience and get the most for their money—but they struggled to "imagineer" anything beyond point solutions.

"They came back with a drawing of the Magic Kingdom without turnstiles," Crofton explained. While this kind of patch might have eased a small amount of customer pain for a short period of time, it was not the kind of bold thinking that would return the magic to the Magic Kingdom. To achieve their desired outcome, the Founding Five needed to greatly expand their horizons.

To focus their full attention on the task at hand, the team moved into an abandoned theater that used to house the Mouseketeers Live Show and got to work. This hideout physically removed them from their daily routines and distractions, and disrupted their calcified mindsets while providing a petri dish in which to relearn, experiment, and grow their new culture. They intuitively knew that, to change their thinking, they needed to change their environment. The Founding Five revised the question, "How can we bring back the Disney magic?" They needed to think big, not apply more Band-Aids, to tackle the systemic problems, patterns, and pain points that were creating distinctly "unmagical" experiences for all. It was time to unlearn in order to radically increase the park attendees' intent to return.

One day, John Padgett was on an airplane, thumbing through the SkyMall catalog. In it, he found a listing for a magnetic wristband, the Trion:Z, that claimed to improve golfers' swings by reducing the pain they felt in their muscles. What if, John thought to himself, everything a guest would need to navigate Walt Disney World was contained on a wristband—from tickets, to hotel room keys, to money for dining and souvenirs and other necessities? What if the team could design something that would give its wearer a virtual key to the Magic Kingdom?

In an article in *Wired* magazine, Cliff Kuang described the scene: "They assembled Frankenstein-like mock-ups using spare parts cribbed from hardware catalogs and torn-down gadgets."[6] By 2010, they had cobbled together a working prototype. They dubbed their creation the MagicBand.

To reinvent the bold future the team envisioned would not be cheap. Creating the new experience (renamed MyMagic+) would require the outlay of $1 billion by the Walt Disney Company.

One of the lessons leaders in organizations big and small need to unlearn is that you *can* do the $1 billion idea—you can and should think big—but to accomplish this, you've got to start small and learn fast what doesn't work and what does.

When you think BIG, ask for BIG, and build BIG, you become too BIG to fail.

The better approach is to think BIG, start *small* (small investment + small risk + small build), and be SAFE to fail.

MyMagic+ was big thinking and a $1 billion idea.

The Frankenstein-prototyped MagicBand (Figure 3.1) was starting small, quickly and cheaply, with the aspiration to achieve extraordinary results.

Together, it was a new way to innovate and a new experience for the executives.

While the strategy to think big but start small was a tremendous step forward in the team's approach, the team still had to sell Disney's

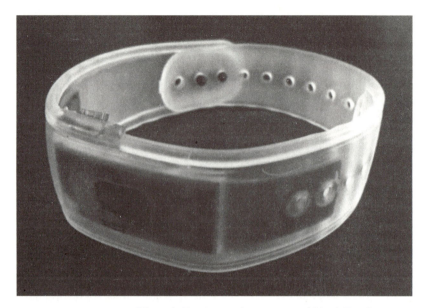

FIGURE 3.1. Disney's Frankenstein-prototyped MagicBand

executive team on the idea, which was anything but certain. Selling MyMagic+ would require overcoming built-in organizational and mental resistance—both within and without—and putting the reputations and even the careers of those on the team quite literally on the line.

But first the team needed approval from the very top to move forward.

In March 2010, Disney chairman and CEO Bob Iger, and the new head of the Parks division, Tom Staggs, visited the team to experience a simulation of the MyMagic+ experience. The team took two prototype MagicBands, put them on the wrists of Bob Iger and Tom Staggs, and then physically led the pair on a two-hour trip through the virtual park. The objective was to safely break the executives' mental model of what the MagicBand could be by letting them unlearn, and then relearn, what the new park experience would be like for themselves. When they came to the door of a hotel room, they might say to the executive, "You touched the door and the door unlocked automatically—without you even checking in at the front desk." And when they came to a restaurant in the park, they would say to the executive, "You just ordered a cheeseburger, and the band automatically paid for it without you pulling out your wallet or your purse."

The team also explained that as people moved around the park, the company would collect all sorts of data in real time. For example, they would instantly know that there's a long line for the Pirates of the Caribbean ride, so they can deploy their staff to move customers through faster. This mechanism would get smarter and better, and inform new ideas for innovation over time.

Both Iger and Staggs were impressed with the team's progress and became invested in its approach. Iger left them with just three (very) motivating words: "It better work."

The Founding Five had demonstrated a new way to lead innovation within Disney. No PowerPoint or promises with only words to back it up. They had big aspirations but evidence to prove the small steps they were taking were on the right path. This gave Iger and Staggs confidence in their vision and strategy to get there. In turn, it made the team feel successful with their new skills and behavior and confident to continue to take the greater and more challenging steps ahead.

Together they unlearned how to do innovation for the park, relearned through thinking big but starting small, and then prototyped and experimented with many ideas to gather the information and evidence they needed to breakthrough. This made the Founding Five and their sponsors confident they were on the right path to succeed.

Once they had the support of senior management, they took the next step to broaden, iterate, and invest a little more in their prototype. The team enlisted an initial group of 1,000 testers who put the MagicBand through its paces. Not only did this approach enable the team to safely discover and fix bugs and glitches in the system—continuously improving it—it turned the testers into evangelists, providing them with more tangible evidence that the vision was real and the strategy valid. Skeptics were brought onboard, and were engaged and inspired by the prospect of playing an individual role in the organizational transformation that the system promised.

The team continued to iterate the idea and build new behaviors across the park—beginning at Walt Disney World hotels, such as the Grand Floridian and Bay Lake Tower, and gradually working across the park to include all 23 resort hotels and 6 Disney vacation clubs, covering a total of about 25,000 guest rooms. In this way, the team was able to grow their idea across the entire park, while mitigating the risk of making just one major bet that *had* to work—that was too big to fail.

Today, more than half of guests entering Walt Disney World do so wearing a MagicBand, and Disney management says that MyMagic+ was instrumental in increasing park attendance by 7 percent and year-over-year income by 24 percent. These are the business outcomes that create greater demand for Disney products and experiences.

By unlearning what had brought Disney so much success in the past, the company's executives, managers, and line employees were able to bring about a fundamental transformation of the guest experience, their abilities and mindset, all while boosting the performance of Disney's theme parks, and the way they do innovation. They accomplished all this while staying true to Walt Disney's original vision for the park: "Around here, however, we don't look backwards for very long. We keep moving forward, opening up new doors and doing new things, because we're curious . . . and curiosity keeps leading us down new paths."[7]

Break the Model, Reinvent Yourself and Your Business

The problem with transformation is never a lack of ideas; it's a lack of a change in behavior. Disney, Andy Grove at Intel, and IAG all came to the realization that if they wanted to have a breakthrough in leadership mindset and business results, *they* had to behave differently, not their teams, and they had to commit to it for a period of time.

You don't trigger a shift in mindset by simply thinking differently; you start by acting differently. When you act differently, you start to see and experience the world differently, impacting your mindset as a result.

Behaving in new ways changes your perspective on situations, which in turn impacts your mindset. The resulting shift in mindset then affects your behavior, and so a virtuous cycle of new thinking and behavior begins (Figure 3.2).

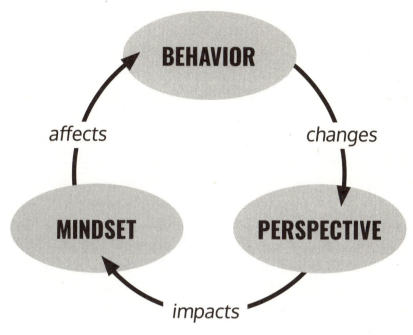

FIGURE 3.2. Transforming leaders' mindsets

The same old strategies delivered the same old results. These leaders decided to take the road less travelled. They realized that unlearning old habits and poor practices takes far more than marginal thinking and action. You've got to be willing to get outside your comfort zone and have the courage to work in new and uncertain ways to achieve breakthroughs and the extraordinary results you seek. These are leaders who don't fear the future; they're inventing it.

Inspired by my experience with IAG's Catapult, I've personally had the opportunity to unlearn, relearn, and break through. I've experienced the magic that happens when you get leaders out of their comfort zone and courageously tackle challenging missions to let go of the legacy thinking and behaviors that are holding us all back. I've worked with $5 billion cargo businesses, telcos with 122 million subscribers, New York City's busiest airport, and others to achieve extraordinary results and provide a lasting impact to these individuals and the organizations they lead. It's inspired me to create ExecCamp, a program entirely dedicated to it.

One of my clients is a large, well-known mobile phone service provider. When I asked the company's leadership team how easy and effective it was for customers to use and get onboarded on their services, every executive told me that their strategies, product offerings, and service provision were impeccable—the best ever. I knew we would have to find a way to help them unlearn what they thought they believed to be true.

I gave the five executives a prepaid credit card—each preloaded with $200—and then asked them to go out and buy a phone and see if they could get connected to their network within two hours. This was the minimal baseline that they expected the company to be able to meet. Only one succeeded—four of them couldn't get signed up for the service: a 20 percent success rate. The experience of going through the process that they had designed and were responsible for, from a customer perspective, was a powerful way for them to unlearn many of the beliefs they had about how the system was working, and relearn how to discover what in fact was the truth.

By relearning new behaviors, such as being a customer of their own products and services, and doing these activities themselves, it enabled their breakthroughs to happen. Giving them a prepaid credit card and two hours to sign up for their own service created a safe-to-fail experiment for the executives to iterate the Cycle of Unlearning. They could then start to adapt their mindset, behaviors, and, ultimately, their products and services, to better serve their customers.

The Cycle of Unlearning can be a powerful force of growth for you and your organization too. In subsequent chapters, I'll challenge you to think big about the aspiration and outcome you have to improve yourself, your team, and your company. I'll teach you how the system of unlearning will enable you to succeed in the face of uncertainty, be courageous, and get comfortable being uncomfortable in order to win.

4

Unlearn

We spend a lot of time teaching leaders what to do.
We don't spend enough time teaching leaders what to stop.
Half the leaders I have met don't need to learn what to do.
They need to learn what to stop.
—*Peter Drucker*

There's an ageless fable that perfectly describes the paradox of unlearning. To gain new knowledge and move forward, we need to first let go of old knowledge that holds us back. In their book *Zen Flesh Zen Bones*—a compilation of Zen and pre-Zen writings—Paul Reps and Nyogen Senzaki recount the fable "A Cup of Tea":

Nan-in, a Japanese master during the Meiji era (1868–1912), received a university professor who came to inquire about Zen.

Nan-in served tea. He poured his visitor's cup full, and then kept on pouring.

The professor watched the overflow until he no longer could restrain himself. "It is overfull. No more will go in!"

"Like this cup," Nan-in said, "you are full of your own opinions and speculations. How can I show you Zen unless you first empty your cup?"[1]

It's easy to pour new knowledge into our cup, until it overflows. But it is important to recognize that to take in this new knowledge, we must first *empty* the cup. This ancient story is a great reminder that in order to unlearn we have to be humble—to empty our mind, let go of past beliefs and behaviors, and make room for the new.

Similarly, if you want to gain new perspectives, new outlooks, and new successes, you must first let go of your old perspectives, old outlooks, and old successes. You must come to the realization that what got you here won't get you where you want to go in the future. Admittedly, this is not an easy thing to do. It requires a desire and willingness to upend the status quo, and then commit to conscious, consistent practice. But I've seen firsthand the tremendous energy that is released when leaders—and the teams and organizations they work within—are willing to set aside their preconceived notions of what it is that brings success, and what does not.

The first step in the Cycle of Unlearning is to *unlearn*—to let go of, move away from, and reframe once-useful mindsets and acquired behaviors that were effective in the past, but now limit our success. There are a variety of reasons why individuals get stuck doing the same things over and over again instead of leading innovation in their markets. The main one is the erroneous belief that doing the same things that bring them success today will bring success tomorrow. Unfortunately, the systems, models, and methods that work today can actually *limit* the ability to change—and succeed—tomorrow.

Our world is a dynamic environment—a complex adaptive system in constant flux—yet our beliefs, behaviors, and mental models tend to be static and inflexible. We are creatures of habit. We naturally prefer an environment we believe we control, that is predictable and certain.

Tomorrow, a start-up that didn't exist a year ago may launch a new product or technology that reshapes our industry, yet we continue to do what we've always done—even as our market share begins to erode. Just a little at first, but more as the months go by. Or we progressively become less effective on the job because we're not constantly evolving our skills to keep up with changes in the world around us. Or we learn from a colleague's feedback that we are considered to be an extremely difficult leader to work with, yet we refuse to adapt our behavior because it gets things done—even as key members of our staff quit for better opportunities. Instead of building systems of work that suit the needs of those doing the work, we build systems to suit how we like to manage. We do this because we understand our own systems and want to control them, regardless of the negative effects on those who have to use them. We naturally hold onto what we know, what we have done before, and what works. Until it does not. And, often, it's too late before we realize it.

This first step in the Cycle of Unlearning requires courage, self-awareness, and humility to accept that our own methods, behavior, or beliefs are limiting our potential and current performance. It's about identifying what we want to work on to unlearn, and then deliberately practicing to relearn it. This allows us to be open to new approaches and to help get unstuck.

The key to unlocking the capability to continuously adapt and affect your environment and personal development starts with *you*. By identifying the aspiration or outcome you wish to achieve—paired with the deliberate practice to get there—you can start to move toward your desired state and achieve extraordinary results.

The Four Necessary Conditions of Unlearning

At its very essence, unlearning is being open to trying new approaches, a willingness, a curiosity, and a belief that it's possible. But to drive it, you actually have to do something. You can't sit there and say, "Great—I want to unlearn." You have to identify a challenge and take action to move forward.

Through my work with leaders of organizations and industries of every size all around the world, I have discovered that we can unlearn the old patterns and practices that continue to hold us back by address-ing a series of specific necessary conditions. These conditions have been validated by the many clients I have led through this process and by the individuals who have applied these very same principles in other aspects of their lives.

Resolving each one of these necessary conditions represents a step through the Cycle of Unlearning, closer to our final destination: break-through.

Necessary Condition One: Identify a Challenge You Wish to Address

Ultimately, unlearning depends on you selecting a challenge—an obsta-cle to remove or opportunity to enhance—that will have a positive effect on your performance. The very first step in unlearning, therefore, is to decide exactly what it is that you will focus your efforts on. Perhaps you've got a long-time product that isn't performing as well as it used to, or your own efforts at personal development aren't bringing the results that you hoped for, or maybe you or your team seems to be stuck in a rut you can't get out of.

If you're having a hard time deciding on what to focus on, consider what challenges you're avoiding, where you're taking the easy option, or when you're not living up to your expectations or can't figure some-thing out. Is there something specific you really want to get better at or go beyond what you feel is possible as far as results? Serena wanted to win one more Grand Slam, Disney wanted to compel its customers to keep coming back to "The Happiest Place on Earth," and IAG wanted to transform what individual leadership and organizational innovation meant in the airline industry. *What* do you want to do?

As you consider where and when to start, don't get trapped in analy-sis paralysis or hold out for the ideal moment, situation, or circumstance to arise—it never will. The best place to start is always where you are—right now. There will never be a perfect moment other than now. Where you start is where you are *today*.

Necessary Condition Two: Define Success as Though You Have Dissolved or Conquered the Challenge

The key to any good experiment is to define success before you start. The same is true of unlearning. But people often struggle to define good aspirations or outcomes. In that case, I encourage them to tell stories of what success might look like if they solved the challenge they decided to tackle. What would they be doing? What might be happening to them, the people they work with, and their customers? How would it be different from today? I ask people to visualize or tell themselves the story of what it would look like six months, a year, or three years after they solved that challenge.

What are the *behaviors* you, your team, or your customers would be exhibiting to confirm that you had addressed that challenge and not only solved it, but dissolved it forever? What would be faster, cheaper, or better quality? Write it down. Doing this will help you start to get a picture of where you want to be, what you may need to get you there, and any concerns that might be holding you back. But the most important part of the exercise is to **THINK BIG**! It's your aspiration or outcome to own, so be audacious with the extraordinary results you will achieve.

Visualizing and telling stories of success in the future is a great way to unlearn your thinking and create a bold vision and definition of that success. Our myopic minds naturally tend to get trapped in the here and now, the problems right in front of our noses. We trick ourselves to believe that if we fix that obvious issue, everything will work out great, but rarely is that the case.

When working with IAG, I asked the leaders, "What would you, your teams, and your customers be doing if you achieve extraordinary results?"

"Well, our customers would be happier," the team replied. "They would have a frictionless experience traveling with us, use our digital products and services more, get onto our planes easier and faster, rebook their next trips sooner."

"Great, but what about you?" I pressed, digging a little deeper.

"I'd spend more time innovating over firefighting, I'd be more productive, and I would spend more time focusing on future growth rather than dealing with the current quarter."

"Great," I continued, "and your teams?"

"We would attract more capable, curious people into our organization who feel empowered to take action and be rewarded for different thinking," they responded.

Similarly, you can imagine the team at Disney would have answered my question with, "Our customers would get into the park faster, be in shorter queues, ride more attractions, be less stressed, and want to return again and again."

The powerful part of telling stories is that we start to describe the *behaviors* that we, our people, and our customers would be exhibiting if we have indeed unlearned. The benefit of describing behaviors is that they are observable, and if they are observable, then they are measurable. Once they are measurable, we only have to quantify how often they would be happening as evidence that we have unlearned.

When quantifying behaviors, I recommend basing this exercise not on averages or totals, but on rates or ratios that are relevant to your historical dataset to support experimentation. For instance, if you wish to leave work feeling accomplished, quantify it. How often would it be happening? Hopefully, not just once. How about four out of five days a week, or even better, 80 percent of the time? Using rates and ratios makes our measure of success more actionable and accountable over time.

One of the techniques I like to use with clients is the 0–100 percent thought experiment to force them to THINK BIG. For example, IAG set challenges like, "100 percent of our customers book, check in, and board our planes by using only our digital products" or "0 percent of our partner integrations will take more than a week." Disney could have set similar challenges: "100 percent of our customers will intend to return to the park after their first visit" or "0 percent of our customers' park time will be spent in queues."

Once we gather our thoughts, we need to write down what we believe will demonstrate that we have unlearned, relearned, and broken through the challenge we are hoping to address. This will help us know we have in fact unlearned. We need to set a constraint—a timeframe, effort, or amount of investment—to hold ourselves accountable as we unlearn our challenge. By setting a constraint for unlearning our challenge, we create a feedback loop to measure ourselves against the results we are achieving and demonstrate evidence we are making progress toward dissolving the challenge we believe is holding us back, flipping opinion to fact. You may frame your Unlearn statements as follows:

I will unlearn *<insert challenge>* before *<this constraint>*.

I know I have when *<list what outcomes—preferably in terms of rates or ratios—will occur to demonstrate we have addressed the challenge>*.

This approach helps you develop a vision of success in terms that matter to you, your colleagues, or your customers. It creates a personal, shared understanding and ambitious model of what better could be, and it sets a constraint to force a feedback loop, so that we can measure our results and hold ourselves accountable to them.

For example, when working with executives and leaders, the theme of decision making always comes up. How to get better at it? How to get their teams to do more of it, not fear it, and let the people closest to the problem—where the information is richest—have the authority to implement a solution to it? I sit with them and help them develop unlearn statements such as:

I will unlearn *decision making* in *three months*.
I know I have unlearned when:

- 100 percent of decisions are safe to fail.
- 100 percent of my direction is what is to be achieved with context of why it matters.

- 0 percent of my direction is how to achieve it—the accountable individual will decide.
- 0 percent of teams I lead demonstrate learned helplessness for their decision-making responsibilities.

By identifying a challenge and describing what success might look like based on the behaviors you describe in your stories, you can start to measure if you are in fact unlearning what is holding you back and achieving your desired aspiration and outcomes and the extraordinary results you seek.

A few unlearn statements for the earlier work example might be:

I will unlearn *stress* in *six months*.

I know I have when:

- 80 percent of the time I go home feeling accomplished.
- 25 percent of my work is focused on personal development ideas.

Many people struggle to define success, especially when mentally trapped in their day-to-day operational view of the world. When this is the case, I offer an alternative tactic: Write down what would be the case if you failed to unlearn, then flip it. If you find it easier to define what failure to unlearn would be, define that. Then challenge yourself to say, "If this is what failure looks like, what would be the opposing success?" For example, IAG decided failure would be only 30 percent of people rebooking with them after a flight. Great! So, success would be what? 80 percent? 90 percent? Let's shoot for that!

Now you've started to unlearn. You have proven you can THINK BIG, and as you begin to relearn you will start small and take the tiny steps to eventually achieve the extraordinary results you seek. But before that, you need to channel your courage.

Necessary Condition Three: Channel Courage over Seeking Comfort

When difficult situations arise, do you channel courage or seek comfort? When you are faced with a challenge, do you duck your head—hoping someone else takes it on—or do you confront it, straight on? If you're not unlearning, that means you're probably staying in your comfort zone: You're doing things that feel comfortable to you, and you're avoiding what feels uncomfortable to you. Seeking comfort over channeling courage often results in taking the easy option of avoiding situations where you feel you're not in control of the outcome. As a result, you're stuck in the status quo and not growing.

That, of course, is a mistake.

Unlearning requires accepting that you'll be outside your comfort zone, and then taking steps to move yourself from only being comfortable in what is known and feels certain to you, to being comfortable in what is new and what feels unfamiliar and not within your control. Accept that it's going to feel uncertain and odd, but you've got to commit to do this to discover the breakthroughs to help you leap ahead.

A major portion of unlearning is the courage to recognize that what you're doing isn't working any longer. It's about challenging and holding up for scrutiny the ingrained assumptions and beliefs that have guided your thoughts and actions in the past. And not just the things that are revelations to you, but also the things that seem obvious. Finally, it's also about recognizing that you're not going to be able to predict the results—that you're sometimes going to fall flat on your face.

Voluntarily moving outside your comfort zone requires *courage*. It requires a willingness to be *vulnerable*. In her book *Rising Strong*, Brené Brown says:

If we are brave enough often enough, we will fall; this is the physics of vulnerability. When we commit to showing up and risking falling, we are actually committing to falling. Daring is not saying, "I'm willing to risk failure." Daring is saying, "I know I will eventually fail and I'm still all in." Fortune may favor the bold, but so does failure.[2]

Brown's concept of vulnerability illuminates perfectly what is required to unlearn—being willing to put yourself out there, to really go outside your comfort zone, and to be courageous rather than to be comfortable.

In her book *The Gifts of Imperfection*, Brown also talks about the need to let go of perfectionism. Many of us—especially those of us who lead organizations—strive to be perfect and for our work to be perfect, when in reality we are human, and can therefore *never* be perfect. Brown suggests that instead of striving for perfectionism, which is impossible, we should strive for excellence in all we do. Why? Because, according to Brown, the pursuit of perfection can actually stand in the way of our success:

> Understanding the difference between healthy striving and perfectionism is critical to laying down the shield and picking up your life. Research shows that perfectionism hampers success. In fact, it's often the path to depression, anxiety, addiction, and life paralysis.

You can (and should) expect that you're not always going to get the results you expect, but that's okay—that's where the growth happens. As the subtitle of *The Gifts of Imperfection* suggests, "let go of who you think you're *supposed* to be and embrace who you *are*."

Pick courage over comfort, bravery over fear, excellence over perfection—every time. I'll take a much deeper look at courage in the next chapter.

However, blindly yet courageously diving into the uncertainty inherent in unlearning will not insure you succeed. While courage is necessary, there is a strategy to embrace uncertainty, and make it safe to fail.

We do this by thinking big, but starting small—tiny, in fact. The important part to keep in mind is that we're not going to stay small forever. Our small steps will accumulate and compound over time, adding up and ultimately contributing to much larger transformations. We build our confidence, capability, and courage with each small step into the unknown as we strive for excellence and betterment.

Where we really succeed is in accepting the small wins with the losses. By thinking big, but starting small we can explore new methods and behaviors safely by creating recoverable situations to achieve the desired aspiration or outcome we seek—as we relearn. Safe-to-fail experiments provide the best way of progressing and moving forward as we embrace uncertainty.

People who find it difficult to unlearn want predictive results, failsafe methods, and the certainty of success. They want to be in control of complex systems; they want results to be what they expect them to be, and not risk their perfect record of success. This mindset and behavior must be unlearned, too, as you create the capability to adapt and course-correct while you discover new insights by performing the Cycle of Unlearning.

Necessary Condition Four: Commit to, Start, and Scale the Cycle of Unlearning

It's not enough, of course, to go through all the preceding steps, congratulate yourself for having done so, and then put your unlearn statement on a shelf to admire. You must take the next critical step, which is to make a very firm commitment to moving forward through the Cycle of Unlearning and then doing just that. But this is not a one-and-done cycle; it is a scalable *system* that allows you to tackle bigger, more ambitious, and more audacious challenges as you iterate more quickly and frequently the Cycle of Unlearning. Each iteration builds upon the previous one as you build your courage, curiosity, and capabilities to strive for excellence in whatever it is you wish to achieve.

International Airlines Group's Journey to Unlearning

In Chapter 2, I described how I worked with a team of six key IAG leaders who were removed from their organization for eight weeks to focus on challenges and opportunities within their company. During this period of time away from their offices and day-to-day responsibilities, these leaders were encouraged to embrace uncertainty, challenge their thinking, and create new neural pathways, habits, and ways to work.

IAG recognized that to grow their business, they needed to continuously recreate themselves, challenge the status quo, and deliberately practice new and more audacious approaches to innovation—doing something radically and uncomfortably different. This message was explicitly reinforced by the CEO of the company, Willie Walsh. He kicked off the Catapult—encouraging the team to challenge him and themselves with a different remit. He shared how he recognized that he, too, would need to embrace uncertainty and new uncomfortable ways of working, and unlearn his mindset and behaviors in order for the Catapult to succeed.

Initially, the team struggled—just as Disney's Founding Five had. They didn't unlearn anything; they just used the same methods they had successfully used in the past. The big breakthrough came after a week of doing what they had always done. We had to showcase their early ideas to other senior stakeholders in the company for feedback and debate. Needless to say, it was a less-than-inspiring experience, but it turned out to be the prompt they needed to unlearn.

We gathered as a team to reflect on our observations and results up to that point. The group had to consider the outcomes they were achieving from their comfortable, predictable modus operandi behaviors against the unlearn statements we agreed would demonstrate we had in fact unlearned.

This was their first breakthrough moment, and the power of the Cycle of Unlearning kicked in, as they started their own unlearning journeys. They became open to the possibility that what they were currently doing was not effective. That light bulb had gone on for them. This realization that their old ways of behaving and thinking were not working was triggered because they were not achieving the aspirations or outcomes they defined. They experienced the result of clinging to the comfortable ideas they presented, and knew it wasn't where they wanted to be.

Once we reached that moment, they realized "maybe there's a better way to do this" and that served to reset the team. They committed to explore different possibilities rather than just doing what they had always done. By forcing the team to think big, challenging their implicit assumptions of what was possible, and aiming for either 0 percent or 100 percent of an aspiration or outcome, it helped get them on the edges of what was uncomfortable and sparked constant curiosity. This willingness to think and try different behaviors is the crux of the unlearn step.

Finally, be willing to commit to exploring in a different way, which for the IAG team was quite a profound revelation. The members realized they could apply new thinking, new perspectives, and new behaviors to everything they thought they knew before. It reactivated their curiosity. Rather than only working in a predictive or operational "just execute" mode, they developed a concept of "look at the possibilities here and let's not be afraid to try lots of different methods to figure this out, fail, and grow in knowledge." They then committed to applying the Cycle of Unlearning to everything they did from that point forward.

The following week the team had their first showcase with the CEO. He asked, "Are there any ideas you haven't shared because you think I'll just say 'No'?" The team smiled. "No there aren't—we unlearned that one already. We took a clean sheet and committed to a new approach!"

5

Relearn

The illiterate of the twenty-first century will not be those who cannot read and write, but those who cannot learn, unlearn, and relearn.
—Alvin Toffler

While the first step of the Cycle of Unlearning—*unlearn*—is about *what* aspiration or outcome you want to achieve and *why*, the second step of the Cycle—*relearn*—is about the *how*. How do you start to relearn? It's simpler than you may believe. You think big about that aspiration or outcome you want to accomplish. Next you start small by doing something that's really easy to do. We take this approach because it enables people to get started easily and feel successful quickly. When paired with deliberate practice, this helps build confidence and gain momentum to take on greater, even more difficult challenges over time.

Relearning is a process of experimentation to try new behaviors and take in new data, new information, and new perspectives. By considering all this new input, we challenge our existing mental models of the world and adapt our thinking and behavior to achieve extraordinary results.

In many ways, we've stopped learning how to learn, so we have to relearn how to do it. Similarly, we have to relearn how we gather and respond to new information—how to see in a different way, listen in a different way, and then be open to changing the way we act as a result.

For example, when working with executives I always ask where they spend most of their time. Invariably, the answer is "I'm very busy and spend most of my time in meetings."

"So how effective are those meetings?" I continue.

That's when their faces sink.

"Not as effective as I would like" is the usual reply.

Researchers have found that middle managers spend about 35 percent of their time at work in meetings, while upper managers spend fully 50 percent of their time on the job in meetings. But, according to surveys, executives rate more than 67 percent of these meetings to be failures—resulting in a loss of more than $37 billion each year in lost productivity in the United States alone.[1]

So why does this practice of ineffective meetings go on—and on and on? Put simply, because people keep applying the same methods they have always used and observed. They become conditioned to what they and other people do, or what they believe brought them success in the past, even though these same methods often won't bring them success in the future (if they ever did at all). They fail to recognize the issue, hold themselves accountable to outcomes, or tackle what they should unlearn and relearn. They don't transform *themselves* and the organizations they lead as the *world* transforms around them.

In this chapter, I consider the mechanics of relearning, including how to reduce learning anxiety with safe-to-fail experiments that enable us to get out of our comfort zones and push our knowledge thresholds further. Edgar Schein, a former professor at the MIT Sloan School of Management, explained that "Learning anxiety comes from being afraid to try something new for fear that it will be too difficult, that we will look stupid in the attempt, or that we will have to part from old habits that have worked for us in the past."[2] I draw on the work of BJ Fogg, a behavior scientist, director of the Behavior Design Lab at Stanford University, and creator of Behavior Design as well as the Tiny Habits® method. Finally, I explore how you can start to experiment with new behaviors to succeed or fail gracefully—and relearn as a result.

Always remember, the best way to create new behaviors—for yourself and for your organization—is to demonstrate them yourself and show people you are committed to improving how you work, how your systems work, and how everyone could work. As a leader, people will follow your example, resulting in a ripple effect across the entire organization. Slowly, simply, and with small steps, everyone starts to relearn new behaviors, opening themselves up to new information, new insight, and new perspectives of the world around them.

This is how we relearn and take the next step: to break through and harness the power of information we gather to inform our decision making and adapt our thinking and behavior, aligned to the overall aspiration or outcome we wish to achieve. Here are the necessary conditions I have identified to take the second step in the Cycle of Unlearning: relearn.

The Three Necessary Conditions of Relearning

Effective relearning requires being very clear on exactly what it is that you want to achieve—and *how* you want to get there. Better decisions? A higher-performing team? Increased customer satisfaction? Whatever it might be, isolate your desired outcome and then quantify it. It's not enough to say, "I want to get better." Be very clear about exactly what you mean by "get better" and how much you want it to increase (or decrease). What are the actual behaviors you wish to observe and measure? Quantify and constrain them. A clear and concise outcome would be something along the lines of "increase customer retention by 15 percent in the next eight weeks," or "improve employee job satisfaction by 25 percent over the next six months," or "reduce our time of ideas to market by 20 percent in 200 days." Your unlearn statement should be audacious, and your first small step actionable.

When you are clear about the aspirations and outcomes you desire, you'll be able to properly explore the behaviors to attain them, determine the right steps to get there, and then know through measurement and data whether or not you've achieved them. Set big aspirations and outcomes, but start with small steps. If there is any question about what it is you hope to achieve, or if your proposed outcomes are fuzzy or hard to discern, then chances are you won't actually do anything different at all—you'll simply default to doing what you've always done, which won't get you where you want to go.

Once you are clear on the aspirations and outcomes you hope to achieve, enlist other members of your team to assist along the way. They, too, will be inspired to pitch in and to become engaged in your efforts— further moving you toward the results you seek.

Necessary Condition One: You've Thought Big, Now Create Options for Small Steps

Let's say you've decided that your aspiration or outcome is to increase customer retention by 15 percent in the next eight weeks. Using the approach I describe in this chapter, you won't try to achieve this entire outcome all at once—this would actually be counterproductive to your efforts and those of your team. Instead, you'll want to outline a series of small steps that will move you toward your desired outcome in an achievable, steady, and sustainable manner. This will enable you to create fast feedback loops and feel successful as you start to see progress toward your aspiration or outcome.

After you have clarified your desired outcome, you then brainstorm options for small steps that will take you toward your desired outcome. List them all. Challenge yourself to create as much optionality for yourself as possible. List new and old behaviors, and those in which you have skills, are a novice, or are simply curious to experiment with. The more options you put down, the more likely you are to find the behavior that will work for you. This is a method Fogg teaches in his Behavior Design training.

Now that you have created a number of options, identify the first small step you believe is aligned to achieving that high-level outcome you desire. Take that small step and celebrate the results, regardless of whether they are positive or negative. This challenges the brain's natural resistance to uncomfortable, uncertain, or unknown tasks as you start to reprogram your neural pathways, engage in new behaviors, and relearn. The simple act of starting is progress, so celebrate it and feel successful that you've started. This small step is your first safe-to-fail experiment, which transitions you to a new way of thinking and behaving.

There is probably no better example of thinking big and starting small than when, in 1963, President John Kennedy announced that the United States would land a man on the moon and return him safely to Earth by the end of the 1960s. This was a tremendously big vision, one that galvanized the entire nation. It was easy to understand, compelling, and *huge*. However, when NASA got to work to achieve it, the organization had to create many thousands of small steps to get there—including the incremental advances required to conceive, design, build, test, and ultimately deploy a wide array of innovative hardware, including rockets, lunar modules and landers, space suits, oxygen-generation systems, and even food for the astronauts to consume on their journey (and systems for them to dispose of their waste).

While you may not be planning to land a human being on the moon, breaking down your effort into small steps will help you achieve your aspiration and outcome, whatever it may be. Work backward from where you want to be to where you are today. What are the steps you believe you'll need to take? What is that very first step?

Consider the Disney team that developed the MagicBand. They wanted to increase their customers' intent to return to "the happiest place on earth," so they reimagined the park experience and worked backward from there. They started small with the prototype of the MagicBand. They progressed to simulated walkthroughs with the executives, and then to working with a select group of 1,000 customers within a subset of resorts, restaurants, and rides, and so on—deliberately taking on greater and more difficult challenges.

Serena Williams wanted to win one more Grand Slam. She started small by working with her coach to introduce new, tiny changes to her footwork, shot setup, and speed of play. Each cycle, each experiment informed her thinking and guided her behavior for the next cycle and the next, toward extraordinary results.

Necessary Condition Two: Find the Right Behavior that Aligns with Helping You Achieve the Outcome You Want

One of the most difficult aspects of relearning is the problem of finding the right behavior to help you achieve the aspiration or outcome you want. In his approach to Behavior Design, BJ Fogg calls this *behavior matching*. The purpose of behavior matching is to find the right behavior that aligns to your level of motivation and ability as you aim to achieve the aspiration or outcome you desire.

Let's say you and I both want to learn how to play guitar. We might go to the same teacher, who teaches us using the same methods, but you excel and I don't. Why is that? It may have nothing to do with the teacher and everything to do with the differences between you and me. You might be, for example, more of a visual learner, while I may be more of an auditory learner. So when the teacher gave us both lessons by reading sheet music, you got it straight away—that prompt matched the behavior of learning music that was better for you. I, on the other hand, struggled because I need to hear music to learn it. The prompt of reading music didn't solve the behavior matching equation for me to learn music.

Behavior matching often requires iteration and alignment to individual competencies, skills, and preferences. It's another reason why you need to experiment with many behaviors because you may need to try various options to find the right behavior for yourself. Doing smaller, faster, cheaper iterations on different behaviors will help people find the one that works best for them more quickly. It's also easier to recover from unwanted results, fail gracefully, discover that it wasn't the right behavior, and move forward if you start small.

People have different behaviors that help them move toward the aspiration or outcomes they want. This is why individual and organizational unlearning is hard—you can't use a unilateral behavior (or set of behaviors) that works for everybody because people are inherently different. You can, however, deliberately practice the systems of the Cycle of Unlearning and Behavior Design to help people find the right behavior that helps move them toward the aspirations and outcomes they want to achieve and aligns to their specific interests, skills, and inclinations—individually.

Necessary Condition Three: Starting Small Is Even Smaller than You Think

Let's go back to my example of "increase customer retention by 15 percent in the next eight weeks." Generally, when I work with clients to determine what small step they should start with, whatever it is they come up with is still too big. They leap to the big single-step solution and deconstruct it into a series of tasks to complete. They don't scale back to small steps to experiment with and grow into. They define success as completing all their predefined tasks, not cultivating new behaviors by taking small steps and course correcting as they progress.

Ticking off tasks for big-bang solutions will not help you relearn; that should be unlearned. Focus on your high-level aspiration or outcome and try to create scaled-back steps toward it. This is what will help you validate your aspiration or outcome, your small step, and create evidence that you are on the correct path to where you want to be.

For example, many people harbor the aspiration to live a healthier life and be more active but struggle to know where to start. Some particularly ambitious individuals have set an aspiration to run a marathon in six months, which for many of us might seem extremely optimistic if not impossible. This ambition gave rise to the infamous "couch to marathon" training program, which promises that anyone can go from being a non-runner to a marathon finisher in six months or less.

So how do you start the program? You'll be surprised (even relieved to know) it doesn't start by getting off the couch and running an entire marathon, or a half-marathon, or even a mile. It starts *really* small, so it's easy to do and start. The program begins by simply getting off the couch and walking for 10 minutes around the block—nothing too strenuous. Then each session deliberately take another small but increasingly challenging step forward, from 10 minutes to 13 minutes, mixing walking with light jogging. By doing this, you slowly and sustainably scale up to a marathon in six months.[3]

When sitting on the couch, running a 26.2-mile marathon in six months is thinking BIG, while walking around the block is starting small, smaller than you think might be necessary to attain your big aspiration. However, embarking on this easy-to-do behavior means you've started, and you can begin to scale from there.

Another key reason for starting small is to make people feel successful as quickly as possible, and to enable them to see the result of their new behavior as they progress toward their larger aspiration or outcome. This is best accomplished by starting *really* small and figuring out how that moves them toward the next higher-level challenge they wish to achieve.

The key to changing your behavior for the long run is to take small, steady, and sustained steps toward your desired aspiration or outcome, rather than large leaps that will be difficult to accomplish and less likely to stick. This means working backward and breaking large tasks and initiatives into smaller ones, each requiring some amount of effort, but not as much as a larger task or initiative.

What are the smallest steps that will keep you moving toward your desired aspiration or outcome, and ultimately to accomplishing it? Work backward from where you want to be, as the NASA engineers did: from a shuttle, from a lunar pod, from a satellite, from a rocket, from an engine, from a spark. Make a list and then make these steps even smaller. Ask yourself: What could I do in a month? What could I do in a week? What could I do in a day? What's my smallest step? Write them down, quantify, and constrain them. Then get ready to get started.

Behavior Design and the Fogg Behavior Model

BJ Fogg has focused his study and research for more than 20 years on Behavior Design and exploring methods and models for creating new behaviors. Relearning requires adapting your behavior by discarding old ways of thinking and doing in favor of the new and discovering the new behaviors that will enable you to achieve extraordinary results. But, as we all know, discarding old behaviors and creating new ones is no easy task, whether in the workplace or in our personal lives.

There's perhaps no better example of this than New Year's resolutions. Whether it's to lose weight, find a better job, pay off credit cards, start eating healthier, get fit, stop smoking, or any number of other resolutions we make each year, most are doomed to failure. In fact, research shows that by the second week of February, 80 percent of these resolutions are abandoned.[4]

Why? In many cases, people take on aspirations or outcomes that are too large, too dramatic, and too difficult for them to do. This slows the feedback cycle, increases the difficulty in making progress, and does not allow people to feel successful along the way. It's far better to break large aspirations and outcomes into small, readily achievable steps that will continuously move you forward toward the success you seek— providing fast feedback mechanisms as you progress. Compounding results builds your confidence to deliberately practice tackling greater and more difficult challenges. Instead of trying to run a marathon tomorrow, start small by walking around the block tomorrow and then building each day from there—small step by small step.

According to Fogg, the path to success is to break down the aspiration into small, specific behaviors using a method he calls Tiny Habits. The key is to make something really easy to do, and then use your existing routine as a prompt for a new behavior. If, for example, I set an aspiration to regularly floss my teeth, instead of starting out flossing all of my teeth two or three times a day, I would start with an extremely small action and combine it with a prompt.

I might use the specific wording from the Tiny Habits method, which Fogg calls a "recipe." For my flossing behavior, the recipe might be: "*After* I brush my teeth, *I will* floss one tooth." Brushing my teeth becomes the prompt for the new habit of flossing. And, after I perform this tiny behavior of flossing one tooth, I celebrate my success immediately—perhaps by looking in the bathroom mirror and saying out loud, "I'm awesome!" Doing this exercise creates a dopamine hit in my brain, reinforcing the new neural pathway. Over time, this habit will naturally grow and expand. As the behavior becomes a regular part of my routine, I can gradually increase the number of teeth I floss until I have incorporated all of them. Success! Then on to the next aspiration or outcome I wish to achieve.

According to Fogg, Behavior happens when three things come together: Motivation, Ability, and a Prompt. These components comprise the Fogg Behavior Model, and it looks like this: B=MAP. As Fogg explains it, "Motivation, Ability, and a Prompt must converge at the same moment for a behavior to occur. If a behavior does not happen, at least one component is missing." Let's deconstruct Fogg's formula and examine each component.

Motivation is the desire or willingness to do something, often driven by psychological factors. According to Fogg, three Core Motivators are central to the human experience: Sensation, Anticipation, and Belonging. Each of these Core Motivators has opposing sides:

- Sensation
  - Pleasure
  - Pain
- Anticipation
  - Hope
  - Fear
- Belonging
  - Acceptance
  - Rejection

Ability is having the skills and techniques required to do something. Fogg proposes that there are three ways to increasing someone's Ability: train them and give them more skills, provide them with a new tool or resource, or make the target behavior easier to do. He suggests that training is the more difficult path. If people are willing to develop new skills, that's great. However, many people resist or resent training. Instead, in many cases you should focus on making the target behavior easier to do. Here are the five factors to consider, according to Fogg:

- Time
- Money
- Physical effort
- Mental effort
- Matching existing routine

A *Prompt* is something external (an alarm, for example) or internal (walking by a refrigerator in the kitchen, for example) that acts as a trigger or cue for people to take action (run out of the building, in the case of an alarm, or have a piece of pie, in the case of the refrigerator). In Fogg's Behavior Model, there are three kinds of Prompts:

- Facilitator (high motivation, low ability)
- Spark (high ability, low motivation)
- Signal (high ability, high motivation)

It's common today for social media companies to send users messages that contain Prompts that are meant to compel recipients to take action. If you're a Facebook user, you know that if you haven't logged in for a while, you'll start receiving e-mail messages from the company that are specifically designed to get you to log back in and use their platform. For example, an email might say that while you've been absent from the social media site, you've received 10 messages from your friends, someone has posted a new picture, and you have five new friend requests.

According to the Fogg Behavior Model, a particular behavior will occur when Motivation, Ability, and a Prompt all come together at the same moment (Figure 5.1). One can visualize the model in two dimensions. On the vertical dimension, you have the motivation for someone to do a behavior, which ranges from low to high. On the horizontal dimension, you have their Ability to do the behavior. Instead of saying that someone's Ability varies from low to high, Fogg conceptualizes Ability as a range from "easy to do" to "hard to do."

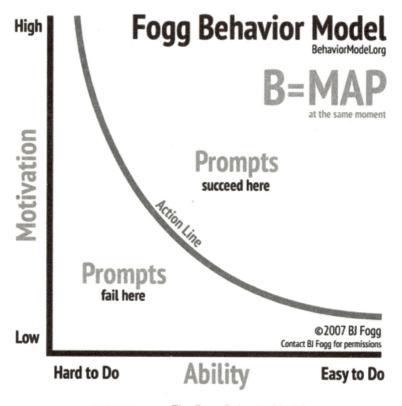

FIGURE 5.1. The Fogg Behavior Model

As you can see, there is a relationship between how motivated people are and how easy things are to do. For example, let's say I asked you to eat a new meal I had been working on. If I told you that it only required tasting a teaspoon of the food, because you're highly motivated by being hungry and the behavior is easy to do, you're probably going to do it when prompted to eat. If, on the other hand, I told you that the meal was super spicy, which you don't really care all that much for, and if you had just finished a 10-course tasting menu and my dish is quite heavy, you are unlikely to eat when prompted.

Therefore, when you're trying to design for new behaviors, it's best to prompt the behavior by making it really easy to do and reduce reliance on high levels of motivation as a result. If something is really easy to do and people still don't do the behavior, you're probably trying to match the wrong behavior to them. They won't get started, and they won't be successful with it.

Of course, there are an almost infinite variety of possible behavior alternatives, and every one of us is unique—we have different drives, wants, and needs. Again, the key is *behavior matching*: matching people with the right behavior, something that they will be motivated, able, and ready to accomplish. When considering the behaviors that might be right for a particular person, Fogg suggests following these two maxims:

Fogg Maxim #1: Help people do what they already want to do.
Fogg Maxim #2: Help people feel successful.

Relearning in Action

As Fogg demonstrates, if you're trying to create a new behavior, then the best place to start is to make something really easy to do. This means that you're not relying heavily on motivation, which enables people to get started more easily. You think big about an aspiration or outcome that you want to accomplish, but you start small by doing something that's really easy to do. First, by getting people to start small, you're creating a safe-to-fail environment, and you enable people to feel successful quickly. Second, by linking their new behavior—the first small step—to the big aspiration or outcome they wish to achieve, you encourage them to feel a sense of progress toward the larger outcome, generating greater momentum, confidence, and success. This deliberate practice is paired with experimentation to find the matched behavior to help them take on increasingly challenging steps, aligned to achieve the desired aspiration or outcome.

Here's an example. Whenever I coach executives, they always have an aspiration or desired outcome to increase their effectiveness. As we commence the Cycle of Unlearning, I ask them to get specific on what effectiveness means to them. Is it better individual, team, or customer outcomes they seek? I get them to tell their future story of what success might look like if they solved the challenge they decided to tackle really well. What would they be doing? What would be happening? I listen for the new behaviors, and then we quantify and constrain them—for example, a 50 percent increase in employee job satisfaction in the next eight weeks. We then decide where to start and what's holding them back.

Identifying and writing down options for small steps that could make them successful—and the obstacles that are stopping them from getting there—is key. Invariably, the topic of the effectiveness of meetings—where they spend 50 percent of their time—comes up. I encourage the executives I work with to add an extremely small new behavior to their existing routine of meetings: to pause five minutes before the end of the meeting and ask each participant how effective the meeting was in achieving the outcomes that he or she wanted. Then go around the room without interrupting and listen to everyone's response.

Adapting their behavior with this tiny tweak inevitably has a huge effect on the overall effectiveness of the team for a number of reasons. First, it demonstrates a new behavior in the leader. Second, it shows a leader modeling new behavior by actively sourcing feedback, measuring their effectiveness, and trying to improve their ways of working. This demonstrates that they wish to improve the system for the entire team. Finally, this can have a ripple effect across the organization because other people will recognize the new behavior in leadership and mimic it.

Doing something small can have a systemic-level impact and network effect, making something magical happen in the organization. As people share their takeaways from the meeting, you get to listen, learn, and test your assumptions of what you believe has taken place in the preceding investment of time together. Did it achieve the intended outcomes? Is everyone aligned? What are the gaps in terms of knowledge and alignment? As people share their viewpoints, new information is shared within the group, and you can check whether or not your implicit assumptions about the effectiveness of the meeting are accurate. This knowledge informs what behaviors you should adapt to improve your (and the team's) effectiveness for the next meeting.

Stopping Behaviors

When we're trying to unlearn, we're also stopping behaviors that we do, realizing that some of these are prompted by very simple things, such as what people say. One thing I constantly coach executives and leaders to avoid is, when someone on a team says they don't know how to do something, automatically responding with the answer. Providing the answer is the most counterproductive response from leaders to the situation. If you want to build capability, you should be teaching the person to problem solve and figure out the answer for themselves—not endlessly giving them the answers. Making people aware of the prompts and the behaviors they perform can also help them realize this leadership conditioning and modify their behavior accordingly.

The Fogg Behavior Model is also helpful if you're struggling to stop a behavior. One tactic is to remove the prompt. Consider the executive's unlearning statement from the last chapter:

I will unlearn *decision-making* in *three months*.

I know I have when:

- 100 percent of decisions are safe to fail.
- 100 percent of my direction is what is to be achieved with context of why it matters.

- 0 percent of my direction is how to achieve it—the accountable individual will decide.
- 0 percent of teams I lead demonstrate learned helplessness for their decision-making responsibilities.

When I sat down with the executive after she wrote this unlearn statement and started to consider the small steps she could take to achieve her desired outcome, she came up with great new behaviors to experiment with, gather new information, and relearn. She started with, "For the next day, when someone asks me what to do, I'm going to tell them to decide for themselves."

Introducing this tiny new habit set a constraint on the executive to adapt her behavior. She saw immediate results from performing this tiny tweak, such as how team leaders responded and who took accountability and who didn't, giving her new information and new insight into what each team member needed. It revealed who to encourage and who to coach. It was safe-to-fail because it was a one-day experiment. However, she discovered a tremendous amount about herself, her team, and the behavioral norms of the organization. All this new insight helped to inform her thinking, make her feel successful in trying something new, and adapt her behavior for the next step in pursuit of the higher-level outcome described in her unlearn statement.

From there, her next new habit and greater but small step was to preface all conversations related to decision making with her intent when interacting with her teams: "I'm trying to move our decision-making authority closer to where the information is richest, the context is best, and accountability lies with the person closest to that situation. Therefore, who do you think is the best person to make that decision? They should decide." Slowly, but surely, she saw more and more team leaders take accountability for decision making, and, in turn, encourage their team members to take more accountability themselves and so on and so forth—a ripple effect across her entire organization.

A couple years ago, I wanted to increase my own effectiveness and how I used my time. I set an outcome to achieve and consider behaviors I should stop to help me get there and I wrote this unlearn statement:

I will unlearn *stress* in six *months*.

I know I have when:

- 100 percent of the time I go home feeling accomplished.
- 25 percent of my work is focused on personal development ideas.

I asked myself what I could do in a month, what I could do in a week, what I could do in a day, and what my smallest step was to get started. I listed the options I believed would help me, the obstacles that were holding me back, and the opportunities I was missing out on. Then I reviewed my own story of future success for the behaviors I believed would help me. I decided that I needed to spend less time on social media; it was something I did habitually that had very little return. Every time I picked up my phone to answer it, check the weather, get directions, or respond to email, I'd invariably end up on Facebook and go down the rabbit hole.

The story I told myself was that I will be more effective with my time, feel less stress, and work on the skills I feel help me grow. One of the biggest obstacles in my way was social media. I needed to remove the prompt for this behavior by deleting the Facebook app from my phone. I still had the prompt of answering my phone, checking email or doing something else on it, but I could no longer check my Facebook because it was no longer there. As a result, I stopped wasting time on social media, and found more impactful things to do with my time.

That, of course, didn't stop Facebook from trying to get me to reengage with their platform. Facebook recognized that I was no longer exhibiting the behavior they desired of me (logging into their app on a regular basis), so they started sending prompts (emails) to compel me to log back in. But because I had low motivation, no matter how easy they made it for me to log in, I didn't do it. I didn't perform the behavior. They should recognize that the prompt they're using to compel my behavior is not working and try another, as their current approach wasn't working on me.

Marketers know the power of prompts, and many apps, social media sites, and online retailers use them astutely to drive acquisition, retention, and revenue by prompting customers to perform their desired behaviors—whether it's logging back in, moving a product into a shopping cart and buying it, or influencing your thinking on critical decisions.

People are different. No two people are exactly alike in every way, so it's no surprise that behaviors that work for one person may not work for another. You and I, for example, might have a similar aspiration to learn a new skill, but that doesn't mean the same behavior that works for you will work for me. As a result, you might have to try lots of different behaviors to achieve the aspiration or outcome you want. This is why experimentation is important when you're trying to relearn.

It's equally important to make it safe to fail so people aren't afraid to experiment. Making it safe to fail is about designing good experiments that create recoverable situations that don't lead to massive catastrophes for individuals or their organizations as they try new methods to relearn. Again, think big about aspirations or outcomes—things we want to innovate—but start with small, *tiny* safe-to-fail experiments that lead to quick progress, results, and new information to help us succeed. For instance, executives lose only five minutes if they stop a meeting early to ask people if the meeting was effective, but they discover a huge amount as a result.

Thinking big but starting small is a great way to help people be courageous while avoiding catastrophic failure if they make mistakes. They tackle the challenge of behavior matching by solving the equation of what behaviors might work for them (or not) as they move toward their desired aspiration or outcome. Great leaders are great experimenters, but they also know how to manage the downside of risk well with safe-to-fail experiments. Some do it intuitively, while others are more intentional.

When leaders take small steps and relearn, it has a profound impact because people then propagate those behaviors up, down, across, and throughout organizations because that's what good leadership behavior and norms look like in their company.

6

Breakthrough

Someone or something always gives up. It is either you give up and quit or the obstacle or failure gives up and makes way for your success to come through.
—Idowu Koyenikan

The third and final step of the Cycle of Unlearning is *breakthrough*. Breakthrough is the result of unlearning and then relearning—it's the new information and insights that come out of the first two steps of the cycle. The new information and insights are extremely powerful because they inform and transform your perspective. You experience the benefits of a new perspective, which impacts your mindset, and you become more open to unlearning your behaviors more often. It's an accelerant.

People find it extremely hard to let go of their amazing ideas. In fact, we are so conditioned to our way of thinking, seeing, and behaving that any new, contradictory, or alternative information that challenges our basic assumptions of what steps it takes to achieve success will be ignored, discounted, and blocked.

As we experience breakthroughs and free ourselves of our existing mental models and methods, we learn to let go of the past to achieve extraordinary results. We realize that as the world is constantly evolving, innovating, and progressing, so too must we. Holding on to the same thinking and behaviors inhibits our ongoing and future success. Our breakthroughs provide the opportunity to reflect on the lessons we have learned from relearning and provide the springboard for tackling bigger and more audacious challenges ahead of us.

This process can be as simple as asking ourselves what went well, not so well, and what would we do differently if we were to try and unlearn the same challenge again. Using this information and insight and feeding it forward to future loops of the Cycle of Unlearning means every loop of the cycle results in deeper insight, and greater impact and growth.

Professional athletes have long known the power of using feedback and reflection to improve their performance and achieve breakthroughs. Traditionally, this insight has come from coaches—just like the ones Patrick Mouratoglou first delivered to Serena at his academy in Paris—but increasingly, technology is providing a very real edge. The NFL has begun embedding radio frequency identity (RFID) sensors in players' shoulder pads to allow teams to gather precise data on their workload and efficiency during practice and games. This near real-time feedback can then be used to help players reflect on their results and gain new insight to perform at an even higher level in current and future matches.[1]

After breakthrough, the cycle starts all over again as leaders deliberately practice unlearning, building muscle memory to push forward with new initiatives, new innovations, new ideas, and new systems of operating. The initial breakthrough leads to the second breakthrough and the realization that you can have endless breakthroughs. What's even better is you recognize that at any point in time, when you need to have a breakthrough, you can apply the Cycle of Unlearning to achieve surprising and potentially radical breakthroughs.

In her book *Mindset*, Stanford psychology professor Carol Dweck outlines the difference between fixed and growth mindsets. She demonstrates the reason why some people believe they cannot learn new information and get smarter, while others believe they can.

According to Dweck, people who have a *fixed mindset* believe that qualities such as talent and intelligence are fixed and cannot be developed and improved over time. In essence, people with a fixed mindset believe you are born with a set level of talents, skills, and abilities—and no intervention or practice can alter those levels. They believe that intelligence or talent (or a combination of both) is what leads to success, not effort, and so they struggle with the idea that they have the ability to achieve breakthroughs and higher levels of performance in any domain.

On the other hand, people who have a *growth mindset* believe that qualities such as talent and intelligence are *not* fixed—they can be cultivated through effort, and developed and improved over time. These people further believe that success can be attained through dedication and deliberate practice, and they are resilient in the face of challenges. According to Dweck, "Teaching a growth mindset creates motivation and productivity in the worlds of business, education, and sports. It enhances relationships."[2] And a growth mindset makes breakthroughs an achievable aspiration for those who possess it.

Mindset also affects how managers treat their employees. Those who manage with a fixed mindset end up with employees who exhibit learned helplessness and never take ownership and risk anything or embrace uncertainty. On the other hand, those managers who lead with a growth mindset develop teams that will take a chance, sensing there is a high level of psychological safety in their team accompanied by the explicit support of their leadership. This encourages employees to seek higher levels of performance through accountability, risk-taking, and experimentation to improve. They are conditioned to take on challenges, strive for excellence, and consistently see potential to develop new skills—and unlearn.

In this chapter, I explore how to enter into and optimize this third step of the Cycle of Unlearning, and how leaders—and organizations—can use it to accelerate further breakthroughs for extraordinary results.

The Four Necessary Conditions of Breakthrough

There's a famous story about an executive who hired Edward W. Deming to spend a week with his team and offer recommendations on how to improve both their own performance and the performance of the organization they led. Word has it that Deming arrived on the first day, said "hello," and then walked straight to the corner of the executive's office to sit down. He stayed there, sitting silently for the entire day as the executive went about his daily activities.

At the end of the day, the executive approached Deming and asked, "Do you have any thoughts?" All Deming said was, "I'll be back tomorrow," and he walked out the door.

The next day—just as he had the day before—Deming walked into the executive's office, sat in the corner, and said nothing. He scribbled a few notes from time to time as the executive went about his daily activities. Again, at the end of the day, the executive asked Deming for his thoughts. Again, Deming simply said, "I'll be back tomorrow."

This cycle continued throughout the entire week until Friday evening, when the executive lost patience and pushed Deming for a more informative answer. Deming asked him one question: "What are the top three priorities for the business?" The executive rolled them off like a shot. "Well," said Deming, "you've spent the entire week working on none of them, yet your time has been entirely booked, and every conversation with you and every conversation with every individual that walks into your office starts with how busy you are. Can you guess why?"

We all love being busy. In fact, we celebrate and subtly enjoy telling our colleagues, collaborators, and competitors how busy we are. The question we don't consider is this: What is the result of all this busy-ness?

In the majority of organizations, being busy is systemic, and often for perverse reasons. Being visibly busy is often seen as or at least equal to hard work, real work, important work. Yes, being visibly and easily observed as busy by constantly running around from meeting to meeting, short on time with places to go and people to see, signifies credibility of hard, committed work. In many cases, people are rewarded for it—further propagating the hero culture of the outstanding employee working late nights, evenings, and weekends to get us over the line. It becomes the drug to keep the hamsters' wheels spinning, and all this motion is mistaken for progress.

It's not.

As we have seen, each of the three steps in the Cycle of Unlearning can be broken down into a series of specific necessary conditions for action. In the case of breakthrough, there are four necessary conditions: reflect, feed forward, scale breakthroughs, and increase your rate of unlearning. Let's take a closer look at each.

Necessary Condition One: Reflect

You may recall from Chapter 2 my story about the IAG Catapult team member who rejected the extremely negative feedback from customers about his idea for a new booking platform he thought had the potential to save the business. ("Customers who really understood would understand—get me the right customers for this idea," he said—quite seriously.) Although the transformation in this leader's perspective didn't happen overnight, he did go on to become the exemplar exponent of the Cycle of Unlearning. He embraced it fully and never looked back.

How did he do this? Through *reflection.*

By consciously reflecting on what had happened, his breakthrough was the realization that the actual issue was *his* behavior: He was telling the customer what they wanted, not asking them what they needed and then designing and building a product to provide that.

For many leaders, the initial breakthrough happens after someone goes through the Cycle of Unlearning once or twice. However, the radical breakthrough leaders discover is when they realize the Cycle of Unlearning is a *system* that can be applied everywhere: "Well, maybe everything I think I know is an assumption, and I should test that. What I should really be trying to do is find the fastest ways to test all the things I do.

And what's even better is not just testing it with myself—I should test it with the people I'm designing for."

I have a favorite story related to this leader. A few weeks after the Catapult, he sent me an email to report on what happened when one of his employees came in to get him to sign off on a new product that they had built. His response to the employee was evidence of the breakthroughs this leader had experienced: "Why are you asking me to sign it off? You should get out of the office, go to the airport to find our customers, and test it with them. If we design and build it for them, get *them* to sign it off *not me*."

One of my clients is a large, global financial institution that was in the middle of a business transformation to develop greater agility across their organization. The firm has numerous initiatives in various stages of completion. But the predominant mindset and behavior of the leadership team at the outset was very much, "We have these big initiatives to do, and we have a big plan to accomplish them. Let's just find out all the tasks that need to be executed and go execute them."

Seems to make sense, right? Because success was defined by the leadership team as completing all their tasks, that's what the emphasis was on—ensuring people, teams, and the company were *always* busy getting their lists of tasks done on time and within budget—and that's how employees were rewarded.

But believe me, you don't break through to transform yourself, your teams, or your organization by simply ticking boxes as you complete your task list. You break through by stepping back and *reflecting* on exactly what it is you are doing and the results your effort is yielding. Are you doing the right things? Should you be doing something different? Are you actually achieving the aspiration or outcomes you intended? Or are you simply ticking off tasks on a list, and asking if it took as much effort or time as you thought?

When I started working with this company, I knew the first priority was to help the leadership team recognize the limit of their existing leadership conditioning to be unlearned and introduce new behavior to relearn. I explained that it didn't make sense to just measure *outputs*. What we really wanted to measure was *outcomes*. So, not the execution-based approach of, "Did we have an idea, break it down to a detailed list of its required tasks, complete the tasks, and then get them done on time, on budget, and within scope?" But instead reflect on whether they were actually achieving the outcomes we wanted from their work in the fastest, most effective way, such as "Did we increase customer retention by 10 percent in the last quarter?" When you frame your work in terms of outcomes instead of outputs, then you've set yourself up to scale your breakthroughs and options for achieving success.

I asked the client team to try a new, small behavior. Before performing work, they would first write a hypothesis for their work—a proposed if/then theory and outcome-based measures of success to use as a starting point—then conduct a series of experiments to test that hypothesis and see if they achieved the outcomes that they wanted. At the end of each week, we would sit down to reflect on what outcomes they actually achieved. This would be their transition from relearning to breakthrough.

The company's CEO quickly discovered that it's remarkably easy just to ask, "Did you do the tasks?" and then move on to the next one, and the next. It's much harder to take the time to find out if the task you did actually impacted the outcomes that you were trying to achieve. During the course of one of our reflections, the CEO wrote on a card, "Agility is hard," which he then stuck on the wall for the rest of the team to see. This was a very powerful—and personal—breakthrough for him. People were shocked to see this admission from the CEO. He went on to explain that he thought he was being agile in the way that both he and the team worked. But then he realized by doing it—relearning why outcomes matter more than outputs—that the way he was doing it, his beliefs and behaviors, actually were incorrect. He also realized how much easier it is to do good experimentation when you hold yourself accountable to outcomes instead of outputs by reflecting on results instead of effort.

While this was a tremendous breakthrough for the CEO, he then went further, feeding forward his insight to scale breakthroughs through-out the entire organization. Following our reflection, he sent an email message to the entire company, who were at the time going through this same transformation initiative. The title was "Agility is hard," and he went on to explain how he was trying to work with the leadership team in a new way. They were themselves experimenting with the practices and principles of the methodologies that they were asking other people in the company to adopt. He thought they were being agile, but upon reflection he realized they weren't. He thought it was easy, but he discovered it was actually quite difficult.

When the CEO came to this realization, shared his failure, and demonstrated vulnerability, humility, and a willingness to work with his leadership team in a new way, he created a ripple effect throughout the entire organization. Not only did he demonstrate a growth mindset and humanize himself as a leader to others, he became a role model for the unlearning that needed to happen in this particular business to build a new foundation for long-term success.

People get stuck just being busy in most organizations. They're constantly being measured on how busy they are, and how many tasks they have completed—the harder you work, the better a contributor you are. Or so it's thought. What would be much better is thinking about what you are really trying to achieve, and asking the question: What could be our smallest effort to deliver the greatest impact to get there? The problem with over-optimizing for executing work is that people get stuck in planning and doing activities—but fail to *reflect* on the results.

They never create feedback loops that allow them to measure the outcomes of their effort, over the output of their activity. They compromise reflection, retrospection, and review of the outcomes of all the output they are creating—the very thought of pausing for even just a moment or two makes people anxious about how it may impact their ability to produce even more output. They stop building feedback loops into their work. They fail to reflect on the results of all this effort or feed forward the information they have discovered to inform their decision making, make course corrections, and guide their next steps. They don't allow time to study, consider, or understand if the result of all this activity is actually aligned to what they are hoping to achieve. They are frankly too busy to. This, of course, is a mistake to be unlearned.

Necessary Condition Two: Feed Forward

As you gather feedback from your small experiments, feed the results forward into your next small experiment, and then feed those results forward into your *next* small experiment—the benefits become exponential. The quality of each subsequent experiment increases because you will tend to apply and compound the lessons learned from previous experiments.

Measure your outcomes over output. Strive to gather feedback in real time to discover rapidly how your efforts have been received, thus optimizing your adaptions and next actions in minutes, hours, and days rather than weeks, months, and years as might be the case with traditional approaches.

These are the steps to take an experimental, evidence-based approach to innovation and build feedback loops in everything:

- Declare a hypothesis for improvement that will address the challenge you're facing or take you toward your desired direction (as you did in unlearn statements).
- Define outcome-based measures of success before starting experiments, and then hold yourself accountable for them.
- Use the information you discover to feed forward and inform your next steps.
- Understand that success is to gather information as quickly and cheaply as possible to inform better decision making and behavior.
- Recognize that the only true failure is the failure to learn, so learn fast.
- Feed forward the information you discover to the next Cycle of Unlearning to create a virtuous cycle that informs decision mak-

ing, new behavior, new perspectives, new thinking, and what next to unlearn.

Necessary Condition Three: Align Impact and Increase Safety to Scale Breakthroughs

One key reason why people can't break out of their old patterns of thinking and doing is because they get stuck in execution mode; they don't take time to pause, think, or reflect. As a result, they don't intentionally build upon effective behaviors and can't scale their occasional successes into greater or more frequent and impactful ones.

So how do we start to scale the Cycle of Unlearning and the breakthroughs that result? The key is deliberate practice, which demands explicit focus, reflection, and taking on more challenging tasks to keep improving and progressing toward extraordinary results. We can begin to accomplish this by clarifying what it is we wish to unlearn, continuing to think big and take the next small step, reflecting on the outcomes we achieve, being willing to embrace greater uncertainty and unknowns, and, again, choosing courage over comfort. It takes discipline to commit to grow and improve. That is why the people who push ahead are the ones who are constantly trying to find their knowledge thresholds, their skills thresholds, and taking one step beyond that. This requires courage because you are not guaranteed predictable outcomes. Like Serena Williams after her shocking loss at the 2012 French Open, be persistent and promote relearning in safe-to-fail ways that provide growth opportunities to embrace uncertainty, accelerate ahead, and win.

We discussed the work of Brené Brown in Chapter 4, specifically her research into vulnerability and courage. Relearning takes great courage, and it requires those who engage in it to become vulnerable to the very real possibility that they may fail. According to Brown, vulnerability is showing courage rather than comfort when you have to take a step into the unknown to achieve an outcome that you want. That's what true vulnerability is and that ties into Edgar Schein's idea of learning anxiety: People are afraid to experiment with new behaviors because they don't know how to do them and are uncertain of what results the new behaviors will achieve and how the results could impact how they're perceived.

We talk a lot about the idea of psychological safety: how safe people feel to fail in front of others, especially members of their team. Google's Aristotle project found it to be the number-one indicator for high-performance teams. People who feel safe to fail in front of one another go *bigger* and achieve *better* breakthroughs. It's not how smart the members of the team are; it's how comfortable they are testing, failing, and being vulnerable with the others looking on.

Google found that there are five key dynamics that set successful teams at the company apart from their less successful counterparts:

- **Psychological safety:** Can we take risks on this team without feeling insecure or embarrassed?
- **Dependability:** Can we count on each other to do high-quality work on time?
- **Structure and clarity:** Are goals, roles, and execution plans on our team clear?
- **Meaning of work:** Are we working on something that is personally important for each of us?
- **Impact of work:** Do we fundamentally believe that the work we're doing matters?

Helping people tie their effort to the outcomes they are seeking to achieve is invaluable. When people can see alignment and connection between their effort and the outcomes they are aiming to affect—instead of simply monitoring their output—it has a profound effect on their ability to recognize how their new behaviors are working, feel successful in attempting new behaviors, realize their breakthroughs, and have confidence to continue to tackle greater challenges to achieve extraordinary results.

This is why it's important for leaders to match and measure people with work that matters—tapping into and leveraging existing aspirations or desired outcomes that are personally important to them and the company—so they can connect their work to the outcome they effect. The desired outcomes must be clearly defined and new behaviors encouraged and safely nurtured. By aligning effort to outcomes, people can feel successful when they engage in the desired behavior that impacts the outcomes they wish to effect. This serves to further accelerate their breakthroughs via the feedback, alignment, and connection it provides (as we'll see with Capital One in Chapter 10).

UNLEARNING PROMPTS

- How do you, your team, and your leadership measure success? By outputs or outcomes?
- Is it clear to you what outcomes your effort is effecting in your current initiative?
- How successful do you feel in contributing toward those outcomes?
- How could you better tie your effort to the initiative outcomes?

If we constantly stay in our comfort zone, we'll stagnate and not grow. By going through the Cycle of Unlearning, we are able to use the results, experiences, and information we discover to make better decisions, and these successful outcomes encourage us to take on the next bigger challenge.

It's important to note that scaling breakthroughs is not about copying the same practices that one individual or organization did to achieve *their* breakthrough—remember *behavior matching*? You scale breakthroughs when you encourage people to share lessons from what they've done to improve, the successes that they've had, and the setbacks they've endured. That normalizes the behavior of getting uncomfortable, being courageous, and embracing uncertainty about how you will try to grow and improve in your own context.

Edgar Schein defined two kinds of anxiety associated with getting outside our comfort zone: *survival anxiety* and *learning anxiety*.[3] He highlighted that anxiety inhibits learning, but anxiety is also necessary if learning is going to happen at all. For example, to trigger change people will often say, "If you don't innovate, your business is going to be disrupted and die, or you're going to get into trouble." That's meant to trigger your survival anxiety into action. In reality, that motivation only works for a period of time—people will eventually dismiss the trigger because while everyone's telling them their business is going to die, they look around and their business still exists. It's not a lasting motivator. It's effective to a certain point but then becomes limited.

The other lever you have is reducing learning anxiety. Learning anxiety comes from being afraid to try something new for fear that it will be too difficult, that we will look stupid in the attempt, or that we will have to part with old habits that have worked for us in the past. Learning something new can cast us as a deviant in the groups we belong to and threaten our self-esteem—in extreme cases, even our identity.[4]

This is why making it safe and really easy to try new behaviors is a tap that has an endless supply of fuel to empower people to constantly experiment, grow, and have impact. This concept ties into BJ Fogg's Behavior Design, Dweck's idea of a growth mindset, and the results of the Google Aristotle project. All of these models highlight the same values and reinforce one another. Your role as a leader is to design systems of work that allow these behaviors to bloom.

Another mistake in business and talent transformation is the rollout of massive frameworks—a fixed set of behaviors and routines—in companies and expecting them to work in every context of the organization. They fail because every organization is different, every context is different, every person is different—again, remember *behavior matching*! Just applying a similar set of behaviors in every situation is not going to make you successful, but it will make you *look* busy.

Let's return to the CEO of the large financial company. As he started to work in a different way, and as he experimented with the way he ran his leadership team, he realized that they didn't actually take a lot of time to reflect on the outcomes of the work that they were doing. By sharing his story—the new insight, new information, and lessons learned, he started to adapt his behavior. By writing an email to the entire company he increased the level of psychological safety for others to be courageous, reducing learning anxiety, and championing a growth mindset among employees. And by intentionally reflecting every week as the leadership team tried to relearn new behaviors, they experienced breakthroughs. They realized they were focused on just doing tasks and not thinking about whether they were actually solving problems or achieving the outcomes that they wanted as a result of doing the tasks.

Necessary Condition Four: Increase Your Rate of Unlearning

The last piece of the puzzle that leads to greater breakthroughs and extraordinary results is to increase your rate of unlearning. Pairing experimentation with deliberate practice enables you to respond to a rapidly changing world. Thomas Edison understood the power of unlearning, relearning, and breakthroughs at his Menlo Park complex, which was known at the time as the "Invention Factory."[5] Edison and his team optimized for the number of experiments they ran, rather than how long they worked. In many ways, Edison's operation looked a lot like today's Silicon Valley tech firms. There was no such thing as a 9-to-5 schedule—workers labored through the night if necessary and slept the next day. Everything was in beta and subject to constant experimentation until they achieved the outcomes they desired and the breakthroughs they sought. Consequently, new products were born.

Da Vinci didn't have a *to-do* list; he had a *to-discover* list. Instead of a list of what to buy at the market—fruit, vegetables, some meat, he would write down questions to answer aspirations and outcomes to achieve. This led him to explore uncertainty and the unknown, and fueled a constant curiosity. Da Vinci's approach to problem solving by asking questions was revolutionary in his time, and it foreshadowed the development of the scientific method more than a century later by Sir Francis Bacon and Galileo Galilei. Here's a brief excerpt from one of Da Vinci's lists:

- [Calculate] the measurement of Milan and suburbs.
- Get the master of arithmetic to show you how to square a triangle.
- Get Messer Fazio to show you about proportion.
- Find a master of hydraulics and get him to tell you how to repair a lock, canal, and mill in the Lombard manner.
- [Ask about] the measurement of the sun promised me by Maestro Giovanni Francese.[6]

Great leaders get better answers because they ask better questions. And they ask them in ways that increases the rate at which they unlearn, relearn, and break through—both for themselves and for others with whom they work and do business. The more times you go through the Cycle of Unlearning, the more experiments you do, the more information and insights you gather, the more effectively you adapt your behaviors and mindset. This will compound and increase the likelihood you will achieve exponential impact and growth because you're cycling through the odds and discovering what works and what does not. Each subsequent experiment increases your lessons learned, which you'll then feed forward into the next experiments, leading to an exponential payoff.

People like Edison and Da Vinci recognized this, and they optimized themselves and their work to go through cycles of unlearning and relearning and breakthroughs as quickly and as cheaply as possible. Today, companies have recognized this advantage. The reason the biggest, most successful companies in the world are all technology companies is because they've built platforms that allow them to discover exactly how their customers interact with them and to more deeply understand their customers' behaviors. They're constantly going through cycles of unlearning what they believe to be true for what's actually true, at a massive scale, and taking a data-informed approach to design their products and services.

Today's most innovative and successful companies run thousands of experiments each year. Amazon chairman and CEO Jeff Bezos says, "Our success at Amazon is a function of how many experiments we do per year, per month, per week, per day. We've tried to reduce the cost of doing experiments so that we can do more of them."[7] And there's no end in sight. According to Greg Greeley, the global VP in charge of Amazon's Prime service, "I would like to say the team thinks, 'Oh, boy, we'll take a deep breath here.' But the way this company [is], it wouldn't surprise me if we continue to keep accelerating."[8]

In 2011, Amazon had the ability to deploy software every 11.6 seconds, which means the company could discover something new every 11.6 seconds.[9] I'm certain that, years later, this capability has only accelerated. And the company doesn't just experiment and unlearn from its website, which started small by selling books. It's across the entirety of Amazon's real estate, including the Echo voice-activated personal assistant, the Kindle e-book reader, the Amazon Web Services (AWS) cloud, the marketplace, and much more. All these platforms support and feed into one another, creating mountains of remarkably valuable data on customer preferences, behaviors, and habits. Their decisions are then informed by all this data, creating powerful virtuous learning loops.

Unlearning is a deliberate, controlled practice. It's constantly pushing everyone in the organization to be courageous and embrace uncertainty and the unknown, rather than just staying with what's comfortable and predictable. And it's always encouraging your people and your teams to discover the breakthroughs that enable them to let go of past success and achieve extraordinary results.

7

Unlearning Management

You manage things; you lead people.
—Rear Admiral Grace Hopper

CEOs, executives, and managers who hold onto legacy thinking and outmoded methods such as command and control—telling people what to do and exactly how do it— are not only micromanaging through control systems designed by themselves and for themselves, they are also limiting the potential of the entire organization. This kills innovation and strips all human creativity, ingenuity, and expression from others' work. Followers gradually become robots simply focused on executing work—not thinking, not questioning, not believing they have any control over what they do. People are squeezed to reduce costs and deliver more output sooner. They forget what it is to problem-solve for themselves, and they embrace disempowerment to the point that having to think for themselves sparks fear.

This learned helplessness halts extraordinary breakthroughs—progress is at best marginal and at worse backward, resulting in perverse outcomes such as the avoidance of accountability or any decision making without sign-off from authoritative superiors. When no decisions are made at the edges of the organization—where the information is richest, the context most current, and the employees closest to customers, the organization grinds to a halt. Executives and managers complain they don't understand why people don't take initiative, but their followers know nothing else but how to follow, never to lead. They live in fear of making the wrong decision, or any decision for that matter; hence, indecision is the result—the outcome that causes the most frustration and dysfunction for all.

Leaders can actually gain more control by taking their hands off the wheel and allowing those employees closest to the situation to make decisions at speed and take accountability for the results. But first executives and managers must unlearn much of their leadership conditioning, which today is still based on an Industrial Era that has long passed. Instead, they must provide clarity of purpose, intent, and direction for what is needed and why it matters, and then stop, shut up, and listen. Let people in the organization with the most context and knowledge of their domains figure out how to get there.

Leaders must leave behind their fixed, Industrial Era mindsets and relearn that they no longer have (or need to have) all the answers—their people do. And for endless breakthroughs to be achieved, they simply need to provide intent and direction, and then get out of the way as people solve the challenges in front of them in ways that are best aligned to the intent they have been provided. The role of leadership is to provide context for what is to be achieved, and why that matters, and then create a system of work that enables people to identify how to achieve those desired outcomes based on the best actions in their current context under their own control.

Your Leadership Conditioning Is an Obstacle to Unlearning

The majority of managers have risen to their current positions based on their competency to know what to do, when to do it, and always having the answer or solution at hand rather than helping others discover the answers and solutions. In fact, these managers are rewarded for this behavior with promotions, pay raises and bonuses, recognition in the company, and ongoing dopamine hits to their brains and egos.

But the higher they rise, the more difficult it is for them to know what to do and when to do it in every circumstance—the span of control is too large, and the mountains of data coming in from all over their organizations too great, and their two or three tried-and-trusted tactics are blunted. The end result of this very common situation is the Peter Principle, where managers rise to their highest level of incompetence and battle to stay there for fear of being found out. They are unhappy and inefficient, and they inhibit further progress for others.

They don't understand or know how to do something and don't recognize the deficit, stagnating in what Noel Burch described as "unconscious incompetence."[1] This is a state that many people long reside in until they can be humble enough to recognize their deficit or be willing to take in new information that highlights it, and then be courageous enough to take action and unlearn—becoming consciously incompetent—to relearn and break through.

Many miss these vital but subtle inflection points to unlearn, failing to realize that leadership is about making other people successful by helping them discover the answers for themselves and guiding them along the way. Worse still, many fail to let go of their past success and situational awareness of how the world *used to be* when they performed that task, role, or responsibility. They fail to recognize the systems and approaches that worked for them then may not work for others now. The world and all of us within it have transformed into something new and different. This is why the Cycle of Unlearning is an effective system to let go of past success to achieve extraordinary results.

One strategy to unlearn your leadership conditioning is to change the environment to stimulate and inspire new ways of experiencing and seeing the world. When we do this, we break out of our regular day-to-day perspective, leave the myopic mindset behind, and immerse ourselves in a new, generative environment. This isn't the annual Innovation Day off-site; it isn't the quarterly leadership get-together, and it's definitely not the week-long innovation theatre tour in Silicon Valley to dream up how to save your business—only to return to the same daily rituals at your desk.

The CEO of the global financial organization I worked with found his breakthrough by making space to reflect on the outcomes both he and the team were achieving as part of their daily work. Yet to achieve this breakthrough they needed to be willing to commit to and acknowledge the necessary conditions to unlearn their own behavior, relearn new skills and new perspectives, and break through many of the obstacles to their own and their organization's effectiveness (which, coincidentally, were often designed, championed, and implemented by themselves). This prolonged, dedicated, and deliberate practice of new behavior built empathy, understanding, and insight into how to improve themselves and their systems of work. And it created a new kind of leader, practicing a new way of leading. At International Airlines Group we took an even more radical approach by taking six leaders out of the business for eight weeks to deliberately practice unlearning. What are you willing to do?

UNLEARNING PROMPTS

- When was the last time you truly unlearned how you lead?
- What prompted it?
- Did you recognize it, seek to uncover it, or be informed of it?
- How might you discover your unconscious incompetencies or the breakthroughs in your behavior and perspective that you need?
- How could you make your unlearning more intentional?
- What is the first small step you could take to get started?

Real leadership is leaving a team, an initiative, or a business—whatever situation you decide to tackle—in a better state than when you started, with new skills, capabilities, and knowledge to cope with the road ahead, even after you're long gone. How many leaders can honestly say they have achieved this? Unlearning management is relearning leadership, and in this chapter, we'll consider why this is required, and how to do it.

The Problem of Legacy Leadership Conditioning

Imagine for a moment that you have been transported back in time to a factory in about 1918, and your job is to lead a group of people whose responsibility it is to manufacture gasoline internal combustion engines for a variety of farm equipment. As a leader at that time, you were steeped in the work of Frederick Taylor, whose groundbreaking book, *The Principles of Scientific Management,* was published in 1911. Taylor's principles, which were quickly adopted by American businesses—from farms, to factories, to small businesses, to government, and more—sought to remove inefficiencies from work processes and to use science to maximize productivity that was measured primarily in output.

In practice, Taylor's principles, aka Taylorism, prescribed the exact steps a worker was expected to perform in whatever job he or she was assigned. So in your imaginary 1918 factory, let's say there is a worker assigned the job of bolting the engine's valve head onto the cylinder block, using eight six-inch steel bolts. Using Taylor's principles, a manager would determine the most efficient sequence of steps the worker should apply to do the job—pulling a bolt from the bin in one motion, pushing it into the hole at the top of the valve head, securing the bolt with exactly 10 turns of a wrench, and then repeating the sequence for the other seven bolts.

As the manager of this department, you know through activity time measurement that this is the most efficient sequence, and that it can be completed in 45 seconds. Now, what if your worker has an idea they believe will make the process even more efficient? You wouldn't be interested in hearing about it, since you assume that the problem has already been solved (by you and some other educated individuals), and the worker is there simply to execute the solved problem. "Get back to work—you're wasting time," you would likely tell the worker. And that's exactly what they would do, or risk being out of a job.

Unfortunately, many managers still live in this legacy Industrial Age fantasy world, where employees are not encouraged to consider new, alternative, or more innovative ways to address problems, as managers have already "solved" them and lost curiosity in pursuing them any further. A worker's role is not to think, just do. Yes, this leadership conditioning and behavior still prevails in the majority of twenty-first-century organizations—and is still taught, modeled, and learned. In fact, for the majority of organizations, their systems of management enforce this behavior, and in most cases, reward it. As Gary Hamel, globally recognized business thinker and faculty of London Business School, once wrote about this turn of events, "Your company has 21st century internet-enabled business processes, mid-20th century management processes, all built atop 19th century management principles."[2]

People model and are conditioned by the leadership behaviors of those before them. These legacy systems of managing must be unlearned.

While that command-and-control approach *might* have worked 100 years ago when only a handful of people in most companies were educated, and the work people performed was repetitive and manual, it clearly no longer works in the world we live in today—a world where volatility, uncertainty, complexity, and ambiguity (VUCA) are baked into all aspects of an individual's role and the workplace. No matter how educated today's manager may be, it's not possible for one person to hold all the information required in their head to build a product, to operate an organization, or to really do the entirety of anything.

One person can't know all that each member of his or her team knows. It's unrealistic, and it's limiting for both the manager and the teams who operate in that model.

Relearning Leadership

Years ago, management guru Peter Drucker introduced the idea of a new kind of worker, the *knowledge* worker—"people who apply knowledge, rather than manual skill and muscle, to work."[3] According to Drucker, knowledge workers can't (and shouldn't) be supervised or managed in the same way that workers in factories used to be. Says Drucker:

> To make the right decision the knowledge worker must know what performance and results are needed. He cannot be supervised. He must direct, manage, and motivate himself. And that he will not do unless he can see how his knowledge and work contribute to the whole business.[4]

Great leadership consists of clearly defining purpose, intent, and the outcomes to be achieved, and then creating systems that allow people to figure out for themselves (by way of experimentation) the best ways to achieve those desired outcomes. While it may seem counterintuitive, the breakthrough that every manager needs to discover and practice is that you become a better and more effective leader when you let go, relinquish control, and empower the people you lead to take control and make their own decisions.

The job of leaders is to design systems that enable people to experiment with potential options and learn as quickly, as cheaply, and as safely as possible while they discover how to achieve the desired outcomes. These are outcomes that leaders and their teams agree upon together, a shared understanding of what accountability means.

When leaders communicate intent, they help employees start to think for themselves, begin real problem solving, and build organizational capability. Leaders can coach and guide teams through asking questions, suggesting aspects to consider, and creating feedback loops relative to the level of VUCA or the challenge the group faces. The higher the level of VUCA, the shorter the loop must be, making the feedback faster, the risk smaller, and the challenge safer to fail. This encourages employees to make decisions for themselves, become psychologically accountable for their work, and learn by doing.

The Myth of Military Command and Control

Whenever I say that leaders should loosen their reins when it comes to command and control, suggesting that it will increase performance and result in better outcomes, someone will invariably chime in, "Hang on a second—the army is a high-performance organization, and it uses command and control!"

In reality, the army relinquished command and control by its leaders in the nineteenth century, after the Napoleonic War. In that war, Napoleon pioneered the idea of *maneuver warfare*, in which he gave small, decentralized teams of soldiers the authority to move around the battlefield and make decisions for themselves based on the situation and their skills.

Napoleon's army was successful in doing this because Napoleon clearly communicated the intent of the mission—the *what* and the *why*—and the expected outcomes to his troops. The soldiers knew the intent of what was to be achieved—for instance, to take the hill from the enemy—and they were given the freedom to determine *how* they would accomplish this outcome, quickly reacting to the realities on the ground and adapting their tactics in real time.

This approach sprang from the reality of the age. As armies became larger—with commanders separated by many miles—communication and close coordination between the units became increasingly difficult, leading to potentially deadly outcomes. Giving smaller groups of soldiers the authority to move on their own, without awaiting orders from on high, provided them with greater agility and a crucial advantage on the battlefield.

This approach to military leadership was further developed by the Prussian Army, and in particular by Helmuth von Moltke (perhaps best known for his saying, "No plan survives contact with the enemy") after he was appointed Chief of the Prussian General Staff. In 1869, he issued a directive titled "Guidance for Large Unit Commanders," which sets out how to lead a large organization under conditions of uncertainty. Moltke explained, "A favorable situation will never be exploited if commanders wait for orders. The highest commander and the youngest soldier must be conscious of the fact that omission and inactivity are worse than resorting to the wrong expedient." The philosophy became known as *Auftragstaktik* or *mission command.*

Under mission command, leaders describe their intent—communicating the purpose of the orders, along with the key outcome to be achieved—and then trust their people closest to the situation, who have the richest information, to make decisions aligned with achieving that outcome.

Unlearning Command and Relearning Control

When starting managers on the path of unlearning management and relearning leadership, I often draw my model of Clarity vs. Competence (Figure 7.1) to frame the legacy behavior to be unlearned and the aspiration or outcome to be achieved: leaders having the *confidence* that their team is *capable* of making good decisions for themselves. The two axes are *clarity* on why they should perform the mission and what's important, and whether the people have the *competence* to make the decisions required to perform the mission.

FIGURE 7.1 Clarity vs. Competence

UNLEARNING PROMPTS

Think of the teams you currently lead or are a part of:

- Where would you place each of the teams you lead?
  Or imagine where your manager would place you?
- Where do you need to be?
- How would you know you achieved the outcome you
  are hoping for?
- What could be one small step, one new behavior, you
  try to move there?

Clarity is the responsibility of leadership. Napoleon tested the clarity of his orders by having one of his lowly corporals shine his boots during briefings with his commanders, knowing the corporal would be listening in on the conversation.[5] Following the brief, Napoleon would ask the corporal if the plans made sense. If he answered "yes," then they would go forward with the plans. But if he did not understand them or was confused, then Napoleon and his staff would make changes or draft new plans that were clearer and more easily understood.

Competency is a capability that can be built up in people by giving them skills by training, tools to use, and safe-to-fail opportunities to practice new behaviors to improve over time. As BJ Fogg suggests, helping people get started with new behaviors such as better decision making means starting small and making it easy to do. Then coach them and increase responsibility as they become more competent. As competence grows within employees, leaders also gain more confidence to relinquish control.

One of my favorite examples of this approach comes from *Turn the Ship Around!*, a book by retired Navy Captain David Marquet. Captain Marquet was made commander of the US Navy nuclear submarine *USS Santa Fe*, the worst performing submarine in the entire Navy fleet. During a routine drill simulating a fault in the reactor, Marquet came to the realization that having just one point of command during the drill made it inherently inefficient, potentially putting the crew and the boat in jeopardy. So except for taking responsibility for launching weapons that would result in the death of human beings—the boat's missiles and torpedoes—Marquet vowed to never give another order. Or when framed as an outcome-based unlearn statement:

I will unlearn *decision-making* in *twelve months*.

I will know I have when:

100 percent of decisions bar launching weapons will be made by the crew.

This meant going against established Navy policy, which outlined in great detail exactly what decisions the captain was required to make, including when to submerge the boat, start up the reactor, shut down the reactor, connect to shore power, disconnect from shore power, and so forth.

Marquet decided that, instead of giving orders and instructions, he would give the people under his command *intent*—and he would ask for their intent in return. For example, Marquet says that instead of giving an order during a training exercise such as, "Left full rudder, steady course 255," he would first tell the officer that his intent was to position the ship near an enemy submarine for attack, and ask, "Where do you think we should position the ship?" The sailor would respond with his or her intent, "Over here," and Marquet would confirm, "Great idea— go there."

As a result, Marquet's officers stopped waiting to receive orders and started requesting and clarifying the mission's intent. They began taking psychological ownership for decision-making and built confidence in their capability to take action without having to always ask for permission.

Marquet moved decision-making authority to the point and the person in the submarine who were closest to the richest source of information required to make that decision. Captain Marquet delegated command and gave control to every member of the crew, creating leaders at all levels. He didn't do this all at once. Marquet thought big but started small. He did this by working his way up what he calls the Ladder of Leadership, starting at Level 1 with the desired outcome for all crew-members to achieve Level 7 (Table 7.1).[6]

Marquet uses the words "boss" and "worker" to denote hierarchy. The words could be "parent" and "child" or "teacher" and "student." At the bottom of the ladder, you have detailed task-by-task instructions for workers to do. At the top, workers are determining what should be done, and reporting back what they have been doing.

LEVEL	WORKER SAYS	BOSS SAYS
7	I've been doing . . .	What have you been doing?
6	I've done . . .	What have you done?
5	I intend to . . .	What do you intend to do?
4	I would like to . . .	What would you like to do?
3	I think . . .	What do you think?
2	I see . . .	What do you see? Tell me more.
1	Tell me what to do.	I'll tell you what to do.

TABLE 7.1. The Ladder of Leadership

The ladder ties into the tension between the learning anxiety employees have about making decisions without clarity, and the confidence they have in their own competence to make these decisions. There are two columns of the ladder—one for workers and one for bosses—to be used by leaders to spark conversations with their employees and encourage them to think and scale their leadership impact. By using this approach, says Marquet, "Together, you will move up the Ladder of Leadership."[7]

As workers demonstrate clarity of intent and competence in decision making, leaders develop more confidence in their capability and step up to the next level of prompting questions they ask workers. Similarly, as workers gain more confidence in their capability, they lead with their statement of what action they've taken based on the intent of the mission. The Ladder of Leadership also makes words like *empowerment* observable and measurable and gives you words to practice and evaluate where you and your teams are.

Under Captain Marquet's leadership, the *USS Santa Fe* became one of the most highly decorated ships in the fleet—going from worst to first to record scores in Navy history for operational efficiency.

One executive I work with from a well-known Silicon Valley technology company wanted to figure out how to grow the company's customer base by 15 percent in the next six months while creating more autonomy and accountability for her people. She was thinking big, so I encouraged her to start small by asking the teams come back with three options, explain the pros and cons of each of them, and the recommendation that they're making—the one they believe *should* be done to achieve the company's desired outcome. The leader would listen and then agree to try an experiment. The higher the level of VUCA, the more she should encourage smaller, faster, safer-to-fail experiments with short feedback loops to gauge how the team is progressing toward the outcome both she and the team are seeking.

The intent was to invest in the best option to increase the customer base by 15 percent in six months, grow the decision-making capabilities of the team, and increase the leader's confidence in them. When a team was highly uncertain about how to achieve the desired outcome, the leader would encourage the team to go out and try lots of different options, run experiments every few days, or weekly, and report back on their progress. If a team had less uncertainty, perhaps they would come back just once every two weeks, monthly, or when the team had made an impactful discovery or needed further clarity.

As the teams saw their leader relinquish command and give them control to decide what experiments to run, at what frequency, and when to report back, they took ownership and became more engaged in their work. Both the leader and the team started small by designing short feedback loops into the process, and as they gained confidence in the results and new way of working together, they accelerated the speed of innovation. They also learned when to seek or share the new information they discovered with one another as a result of rapidly experimenting—using the new information to course-correct, validate, or update their direction and innovate at speed. The group didn't achieve the 15 percent increase in six months; they did it in 16 weeks. This is how you can start small to unlearn management and relearn leadership at all levels.

Control is created not by telling people what to do but by designing feedback loops into the system of work to help teams measure against the outcomes they're achieving, how they're moving toward them, and what they're learning along the way.

Introducing a fundamental behavior like this is not easy for someone whose leadership conditioning has been to own command and hold onto control by telling people *what* and *how* to do their work. It will feel unsettling and uncomfortable, and there's always the chance that this discomfort will persuade you to go back to your old ways of leading. But if you persevere and give up control to your people—one small step up the Ladder of Leadership, one small step at a time—you will create greatness in others, which is the best possible outcome for any leader, especially at scale.

The Flow Zone

There are many ways to model the transition to relearning leadership control and to letting go, but one I find particularly interesting is dynamic difficulty adjustment, an idea that came from the world of video game development. When people design a video game, they want players to enjoy and become engaged in the experience. If a game is too complex or too difficult, players will become frustrated or anxious, causing them to quit in a short amount of time. If a game is too easy, then players will become bored and also quit in a short amount of time. The ideal outcome is to design a game that isn't so complex or difficult that it causes players to quit, but that is interesting or challenging enough to avoid causing players to get bored.

In Figure 7.2, this ideal outcome is illustrated in the *flow zone*, which refers to Mihaly Csikszentmihalyi's idea of *flow*—"a state in which people are so involved in an activity that nothing else seems to matter; the experience is so enjoyable that people will continue to do it even at great cost, for the sheer sake of doing it." The flow zone shows where challenge and ability are balanced, and flow naturally occurs.

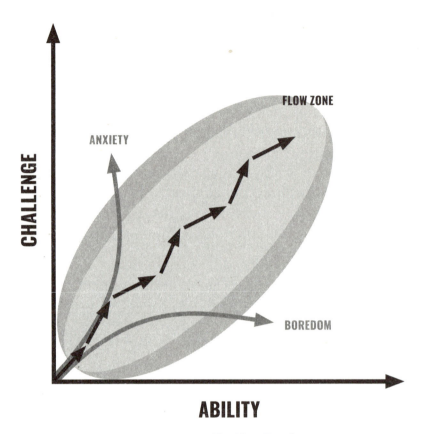

FIGURE 7.2.   The Flow Zone[8]

According to Csikszentmihalyi, there are eight characteristics of flow:

- Complete concentration on the task.
- Clarity of goals and reward in mind and immediate feedback.
- Transformation of time (speeding up/slowing down of time).
- The experience is intrinsically rewarding.
- Effortlessness and ease.
- There is a balance between challenge and skills.
- Actions and awareness are merged, losing self-conscious rumination.
- There is a feeling of control over the task.[9]

However, people are different, and what one player finds complex, difficult, and frustrating, another player will find simple, easy, and boring. Flow is broken, and the game player quits. What is a game designer to do?

They create interactive video games, such as Candy Crush, that incorporate *dynamic difficulty adjustment*—a system that scales the difficulty of the game up or down in real time, depending on the player's skill level. While this might seem on the surface to be commonsensical, it requires the designer to do something he or she might not want: to give up control over how the game is played and delegate this crucial duty to the software itself.

Games provide safe-to-fail environments for people to unlearn, relearn, and break through. This is why the military runs simulations and war games, and why gamers keep playing and playing games to develop their skills and improve. Augmented reality (AR) and virtual reality (VR) will only accelerate this process in the future.

The concept of dynamic difficulty adjustment can be applied to a leadership setting. Some people find certain behaviors easy, while others find the same behaviors hard. This ties back to the axes of clarity and competence—clarity of intent (and confidence in what decision needs to be made) and the competence of taking action, based on the capability, skill level, and experience they have from making those decisions before. The idea is to develop everyday employees so they feel confident and capable of making decisions and taking the lead themselves—without the constant command and control of the organization's leaders. But leaders must feel confident and the team must be capable for them to delegate decisions down to the appropriate person. Both parties have to work their way into the zone.

When you encourage people to start thinking and making decisions for themselves, or you start asking questions to see if they understand the mission's intent—and they reply with their intent—you get evidence that you're developing confidence and capability and moving up the Ladder of Leadership by unlearning management and relearning leadership.

When you start to ask questions like, "What do you think we should do?" others start to build psychological ownership and accountability because *they're* making the decision. They start explaining what it is they're trying to do, and why they have decided to do it—their own intent. Your job as a leader is to let go of your legacy behavior and create a system that allows and supports your people to make good decisions themselves, for which you provide clarity of intent and seek to build the competence for others to provide their intent in return.

Alan Mulally, who served as CEO of Boeing Commercial Airplanes and Ford Motor Company (he turned the latter around from a $17 billion loss to profitability), used his Working Together Management System to manage both companies. The system involved gathering together his top managers every week to review their business plan and to identify any problems. When a problem was identified, managers were required to find the people in the company closest to the problem and who were in the best position to solve it. Mulally firmly believed that the job of his leadership team was not to solve every problem. Instead, it was to identify problems and then find the people most qualified to solve them.

To unlearn Industrial Era management and command and control, relearn leadership, and break through to this intent-based world, leaders have to embrace the Cycle of Unlearning to identify ways that they can slowly start to let go of giving every command and controlling every decision. To accomplish this requires being confident in the capability of the people who report to them to competently take control of the decisions that need to be made. This is one of the most important problems I come up against, especially when working with leaders. They have a mindset and conditioning that the reason they've become a leader or a manager in the company is because they knew all the answers—that was the foundation of their competence. So when people would ask them questions, they felt they had to have the answer to demonstrate their competence and maintain command by exercising control.

While it feels good to get the dopamine hit when you have the correct answer, it prevents the discovery of new options and it makes it unnecessary for other people to think, creating the learned helplessness that renders people fearful of making any decisions at all. Worse, it stops people from even contributing.

One of the things I do as a consultant is to help leaders get out of the business of making decisions and get into the business of helping others make good decisions that are aligned with the intent that they're trying to move toward. It's a subtle but very powerful shift. This is what leaders must unlearn, and then relearn, with safe-to-fail opportunities for them and their people they lead to develop confidence and capability together, if they want to be more effective, more successful, break through, and achieve extraordinary results.

Relearn to Move Decisions to the Information

Some believe that you're either born a leader or not, and if you're not born a leader, then you can never be all that good as one and you shouldn't even try. This, of course, is rubbish, and grounded in the fixed mindset described by Carol Dweck. There are systems that allow anyone to discover how to be a good leader—perhaps even a *great* one.

This is one of the premises that I have to teach people all the time. High-performance individuals and companies create systems that allow the people closest to the richest sources of information to have the authority to make decisions, because they have the most context of the situation and the competence of skills required for how best to take action. Moving authority to the appropriate individual is what creates the accountability. Leadership responsibility is to clarify the desired outcomes, not the individual's actions.

It's important to note that leaders don't just randomly trust their people. Individuals and organizations create systems that give them trust or fast feedback, if the aspiration or outcome they wish to achieve is not possible, flawed, or must be corrected—thus providing control. This requires creating and scaling systems of work that encourage people to take responsibility and accountability by giving them opportunities to run safe-to-fail experiments with tight feedback loops. This allows leaders to relinquish command when they see evidence of competence in their employees, and they gain confidence in their ability to make good decisions and take control. This is the environment high performers don't only thrive in—they seek it.

There's a great story that Adrian Cockcroft, VP of Cloud Architecture Strategy at Amazon Web Services, tells about the time he was at Netflix. Adrian was in a meeting with a group of senior executives from major banks, retailers, and others, and the executives complained that they were unable to do the same level of innovation because they didn't have great engineers like Netflix did. Adrian looked around the table and saw the names of all the companies in attendance. His reply was, "But we got them from you! We just create an environment where we told them what we wanted, and got out of their way to achieving it."

In some respects, the management innovation that I'm asking my clients to unlearn is to stop making decisions and let other people make decisions. Toyota has long believed that first-line employees can be more than cogs in a soulless manufacturing machine; they can be problem solvers, innovators, and change agents. While American companies relied on staff experts to come up with process improvements, Toyota gave every employee the skills, the tools, and the permission to solve problems as they arose and to head off new problems before they occurred. Toyota's real advantage was its ability to harness the intellect of "ordinary" employees. In fact, if you ask executives what Toyota does, they won't say they build cars; they'll say they build great people who build great cars.

Toyota pioneered the use of *Andon cords* strung above the assembly lines in their manufacturing plants; now wireless yellow call buttons serve the same purpose.[10] When there is a serious problem that can't be quickly and easily resolved, assembly line workers have the authority to push the yellow call button, which immediately stops the assembly line of the entire factory and illuminates a sign above the workstation, which indicates exactly where the problem is.

When an employee pushes the button, the first thing the manager does is "go-and-see" the problem immediately by stopping whatever he or she is doing and physically walking over to the workstation in question—not making a call to the workstation from his or her office on the executive floor or sending an email demanding action and answers. A key element in Toyota's Production System and work process is that the managers actually go to the workstations where the problems are to see it for themselves. The managers thank employees for finding the problems, and then ask the workers a series of five questions to aid the employees in problem solving to address the obstacle they have discovered. In his book *Toyota Kata*, Mike Rother describes this as the Coaching Kata:

1. What is the target condition?
2. What is the actual condition now?
3. What obstacles do you think are preventing you from reaching the target condition? Which one are you addressing now?
4. What is your next step (next experiment)? What do you expect?
5. When can we go and see what we have learned from taking that step?

The managers don't tell the employees how to fix the problem or correct it for them. Instead, they work together to devise an experiment that improves the system of work.

It's not about the leader solving the problem. It's about coaching the employee to improve their capability and competency of doing the work, so they can better solve problems. And it requires employees to think and come up with different options, examine them, explain their intent, and the upsides and downsides of each of the options. What's the potential benefit of each? What's the potential cost or impact? As a leader, your role is to teach employees how to evaluate the various options and develop a position about what they think should be done.

The question for leaders is how they can move decision making to the appropriate individual and have the confidence necessary to delegate authority. The journey starts small: to manage uncertainty by way of the feedback loops you design into your systems of work, then building both your own and the team's confidence and capabilities to explore problems and figure them out.

Amazon's Leadership Principles: Scaling a System of Confidence and Capability of Leadership

Amazon Web Services (AWS) has set the bar high for the provision of innovative public cloud services to some of today's largest and most successful companies. In the final quarter of 2017 (Q4 2017), AWS's revenue surged to $5.11 billion—a revenue growth rate of 44.6 percent, taking AWS revenue to $17.46 billion for the year and accounting for approximately 10 percent of Amazon's entire revenue for 2017.[11] Long story short, AWS continues to ward off an array of competitors in the cloud, including Microsoft and Google.

I am convinced that a significant reason for AWS's success, and for the continued success of Amazon overall, is its approach to leadership. This approach to scaling their system of leadership—which among other things pushes decision making down from leaders to employees—is baked into Amazon's leadership principles. These principles represent the organizational intent of the company and how to respond to any situation. Everyone in Amazon is expected to follow these principles. It is a codification of their behavioral norms. It is not just for "leaders," as everyone in the organization is considered to be a leader in whatever it is they do. What follows are a few examples (all of the principles can be found here at amazon.jobs/principles).

Learn and Be Curious

Leaders are never done learning and always seek to improve themselves. They are curious about new possibilities and act to explore them.

Think Big

Thinking small is a self-fulfilling prophecy. Leaders create and communicate a bold direction that inspires results. They think differently and look around corners for ways to serve customers.

Bias for Action

Speed matters in business. Many decisions and actions are reversible and do not need extensive study. We value calculated risk taking.

Earn Trust

Leaders listen attentively, speak candidly, and treat others respectfully. They are vocally self-critical, even when doing so is awkward or embarrassing. Leaders do not believe their or their team's body odor smells of perfume. They benchmark themselves and their teams against the best.

Have Backbone; Disagree and Commit

Leaders are obligated to respectfully challenge decisions when they disagree, even when doing so is uncomfortable or exhausting. Leaders have conviction and are tenacious. They do not compromise for the sake of social cohesion. Once a decision is determined, they commit wholly.[12]

This subset of Amazon's principles is a way to create a system that allows people to make decisions that are aligned with what the company values and its leadership intent. There's nothing that says employees should launch a new product or service—or not. The principles provide the dynamics to challenge employee thinking at every level.

As you build your own system, define intent of what great leadership is and then hold one another accountable to it. This will enable you to scale the system of leadership to your entire organization—566,000 people in Amazon's case.[13]

Great Systems of Leadership Lead Themselves

When leaders and teams create great systems and behavioral norms, people want to protect them. And one of the best ways to protect these systems is to ensure that the people you hire and retain in the organization are aligned with the intent of your systems—and remove those that aren't. If someone doesn't value what the system values, then he or she is not the correct member for the system—for your organization.

One of my favorite stories that exemplifies this is the hiring process for surgeons at the Mayo Clinic. The Mayo Clinic attracts some of the top medical practitioners and surgeons in the United States and internationally, which provides the clinic with a remarkably talented pool of candidates to draw from. What separates one top surgeon from another is less technical and more behavioral, and the clinic ardently searches for team players in its hiring.

To help determine which of these many talented individuals is most likely to fit in Mayo's organizational culture, the members of the interview team always ask this question: "Tell us about the most difficult surgery you've performed." And then they listen closely to the surgeon's response—counting how many times they say "I" versus "we." If the ratio of "I" to "we" is over a certain amount, the surgical candidate won't be offered a position at the Mayo Clinic. The belief is that surgery is such a complex and difficult task that no one person can do it on his or her own. Surgeons need a great team to support them. That is the system that Mayo Clinic values, and candidates who aren't aligned with the system are rejected to ensure that it is protected.

In his book *Principles: Life and Work*, investor and entrepreneur Ray Dalio presents six principles for getting the culture right in any organization. These principles are based on the application of hedge fund quantitative thinking and computerized machine learning processing to decision-making processes in human systems. They have their own system of leadership based on clarity and competence captured in the principles they value:

- Trust in radical truth and radical transparency.
- Cultivate meaningful work and meaningful relationships.
- Create a culture in which it is okay to make mistakes.
- Get and stay in sync.
- Believability weight your decision making.
- Recognize how to get beyond disagreements.[14]

Dalio aims for radical transparency about how people get to the decisions they want. He asks the question, "Instead of saying I'm right, how could I create a system to help me know if I was right?" The answer is to use radical transparency, real-time colleague feedback, and algorithmic processing power to create an idea marketplace where people are encouraged to speak up, tell the truth, and have their believability rated and ranked to inform the group decision making.

In one example, Dalio has a system for meetings where people receive real-time feedback from other people in the meeting about how they are performing. So I might be in a meeting talking about leadership, and other meeting participants will be asked, "On a scale of one to ten, how believable is Barry right now?" And you get that real-time feedback from everyone in the meeting. It's radical transparency, but it's also a data-informed, automated approach; people are providing feedback and collecting data as you're going.

The end result is an automated system of leadership and an environment where people can make decisions based on others' demonstrated confidence and capability. While it may not be for everyone, it shows how human systems can and are being augmented with technology, in search of higher performance.

By helping your people get better at making decisions, you can get better at letting go of making all the decisions yourself. Great leaders provide clarity of intent and the outcomes to be achieved, and they build competence in their people to be confident and capable in making those decisions. For most leaders, this requires unlearning the way they lead, and letting go of making all the decisions.

What we're trying to do is move decision-making authority and accountability to where the information is richest, and to the people closest to it. The reason many companies are slow and languid is because employees aren't allowed to make decisions. They have to have meetings and run their ideas up and down the chain of command. They have to get through a jungle of bureaucracy and red tape, just to get in front of a leader for a sign-off—or a rejection. Whatever the decision turns out to be, the process is too slow. What you really want leaders to do is communicate the outcome and then let the teams make the decisions on how best to get there—just like mission command.

This requires leaders taking their hands off the wheel. You might think that's too great a leap to make—that there's too much at risk—but you can think big, start small, and teach your teams how to make good decisions. When you have decisions that are highly uncertain, make feedback loops shorter and faster, gather information, adjust, and go again. Fundamentally, it comes down to unlearning your legacy leadership conditioning and relearning the better behaviors that will make you a better leader and make your people better leaders, too. The breakthrough occurs when you've got all your people leading, and they're scaling the leadership in your organization.

You can't do it by yourself, but with everyone rowing as one, with a singular mind, you can scale your leadership—and your ability to do more, deliver greater impact, and grow.

8

Unlearning with Customers

*I like to listen. I have learned a great deal from
listening carefully. Most people never listen.*
—Ernest Hemingway

Ultimately, all the things we do in business are for the customer. Unfortunately, as we keep our noses firmly planted to the grindstone, we tend to lose sight of our customers, their needs and desires. This is especially true for customers who quietly send us their money without complaint. We take them for granted, forgetting how to excite them and turn them into our greatest fans and strongest sales team.

For the majority of companies, engaging customers and obtaining their feedback comprises the last step in the product journey. After we have spent significant time and money designing, building, and launching new products, services, or processes for our customers, it's often only then that we ask them what they think. Unfortunately, this is absolutely the worst moment to first hear what our customers have to say—it's far too late.

We must unlearn the way we engage, collaborate, and create with our customers, and relearn how to interact, leverage, and connect with them to discover new innovations and breakthroughs together. T-Mobile CEO John Legere understands this better than most leaders. When Legere first joined the company in 2012, he didn't sit in his office and consume endless presentations made by employees, market analysts, and researchers. Instead, he did the work himself. He had a special phone line installed in his office to listen directly to customer service calls for three hours a day and better understand what obstacles, issues, and challenges customers were facing while trying to use T-Mobile's services. Says Legere, "I use it every day, and especially in the beginning it gave me great insight into customer pain points."[1]

In this way, he created an unfiltered and unsanitized firehose of customer feedback to inform what both he and T-Mobile needed to unlearn and relearn in order to improve their customers' experience and innovate T-Mobile's products and services. Legere gained pure insight from the people who live and breathe T-Mobile's products and services every day, and who know what it does well and what it does not.

He also personally uses social media (Legere currently has millions of Twitter followers) to receive customer feedback in near-real time, and then take immediate action in response. In an interview, Legere explained, "I'm constantly in touch at a moment's notice with my customers and everybody else's customers. I can learn exactly what's going on—I get great feedback." According to Legere, he *always* replies personally when someone sends him a message.

Most executives rarely speak with customers, never mind a low-ranking employee. In fact, the thought of it fills them with fear. They prefer to hold court, hide behind their hardwood desks, and believe they know best for the business based on their many years in the industry. They lack the vulnerability, transparency, and curiosity to discover the real results of their strategies. More important, the last people they want to hear feedback from are those for whom they are apparently designing products and services.

We have much to learn from our customers if only we are willing to listen, and listen we must if we are to succeed. Today's technology allows us new ways to receive customer input immediately, take action, and positively affect and improve our methods instantly. Feedback is most effective when it comes from reality, and the reality provided by our customers far exceeds the opinion of any internal authority figure. In this chapter, we'll take a deep dive into this topic and see what lessons can be applied to your own organization.

How Do You Gather Information to Unlearn?

One of the best mechanisms we have for recalibrating our perspective of the world, making our unconscious incompetence visible, and for checking if what we believe to be true is actually true, is soliciting candid feedback from our customers and then putting it to use. Why, then, do organizations—and the men and women who run them—do such a poor job of it?

Whether you're an executive in a large organization, the founder of a one-day-old start-up, or somewhere in between, you're responsible for creating a vision and a strategy to achieve that vision for your company. A vision is a belief, and so are the strategies you deploy to achieve it. They are both hypotheses of what you believe to be true, and the way you realize and test both the vision and strategy of your company is through the products or services you build. The feedback you gather on all these elements helps you discover the information you need to succeed.

Therefore, how we gather information—especially from our customers, through their experience of the product and services we create—becomes the key input for our Cycle of Unlearning, to understand what works and what does not. It helps us identify what we may need to unlearn and relearn, and know when we have achieved the breakthroughs that lead to extraordinary results.

The success or failure of your products and services is dependent on how effectively you gather information from customers and other stakeholders on how they are performing. This feedback also determines how well you unlearn the limiting aspects of those products and services, relearn how to improve them, and leverage those insights to break through toward the extraordinary results that enable your company to leap into the lead.

Today's most effective leaders wholeheartedly embrace the idea of removing the friction in how they communicate with customers, so they are able to solicit and receive a steady, raw feed of unsanitized information and data that is true, accurate, and as close to real time as possible. They can make better decisions based on insights from real customers *outside* the organization. This feedback is invariably better, less biased, and richer than the reports that well up from within the company and the market analysis and research, which is generally just an outsourced collection of people's opinions. It also opens them up in a variety of interesting ways to test their beliefs to unlearn, relearn, and break through, and then adapt their mental models and behaviors as necessary.

Do You Know Who Your Customers Are?

Companies (and the executives who run them) really have two customers to consider and serve. First, there are the traditional customers that you would consider outside the organization, the customers for the products and services that you build and sell to the world at large. When you're talking about building a culture and operating processes in your organization, however, there's a second customer: the employees for whom you design systems of work and the processes that go along with them. They are customers because they are the ones who are impacted by the culture and operating processes leadership has designed and built on a day-to-day basis. You need to incorporate the feedback of *all* your customers—both internal and external—to understand how the business is working, how the products and services you're delivering are working, and how both can be improved.

Relearning How to Get the Information to Unlearn

When I first start working with an executive or leader, one of the first steps I take is to review a list of all the initiatives that are going on in their organization at that moment, along with their reporting dashboards. I go through their boards, and invariably, there are maybe one or two problems raised, but the majority of initiatives are going well—at least as far as the reporting dashboards indicate. That's when I tell the executive, "I'm fairly certain that what you've got here is a watermelon report."[2] What I mean by that is that it's green on the outside, but red on the inside. That is, people report that everything's fine, but deep down they know it's not.

What happens is that the information gets sanitized, often filtered and massaged by teams and individuals who are disconnected from their customers and fearful of management, but reporting information up the organization. As a result, leaders end up making poor decisions based on poor information. One reason for poor information is when employees are fearful of sharing negative outcomes—a key indicator that psychological safety is low and learning anxiety is high. As Deming said, "Whenever there is fear, you will get wrong figures."[3]

Addressing these issues and indicators is the responsibility of leadership, the key test being how you as a leader respond to negative outcomes and critical feedback. Is it an opportunity to improve the system or an excuse to blame the individual? Which part of Westrum's culture model are you championing—pathological, bureaucratic, or generative?

When leaders make bad decisions based on bad information, it leads them—and the companies they work for—in a terrible direction.

One other question I often ask executives is: "How do you solicit that information? Do you communicate solely through reports going up and down through multiple layers of management in the company? In my experience, most leaders' default conditioning is to build or maintain layers of supervisors and managers, which creates communication handover points. These handover points always lead to slow decision making, poor collaboration, and loss of context as what's actually happening in the organization gets lost in the message.

There's a significant impact. For example, when I was coaching a senior executive team of a very large retailer, the executives all worked on the twenty-first floor of the building, a place where few employees had ever ventured. There were security officers, you needed special keys to take the elevator up there, and you could only visit if you were invited or *summoned* by an executive. The only people up there on the twenty-first floor were executive vice presidents and above. These executives had totally removed themselves, not only from their external customers but also from their internal customers—their employees—and from any real information that was traveling through their company.

This is the reality on the ground for many executives who live in their ivory office towers, totally disconnected from what's going on—both inside and outside the organization. The result is poor decision making based on inadequate, missing, or outright inaccurate information that they're gathering (or, more likely *not* gathering) themselves or being told by their people. This leads to negative effects throughout their organizations.

As leaders, each of us must start thinking about unlearning how we gather information to inform our beliefs and challenge our mental models and behaviors. We need to be curious if we hope to close the gap between what we think we're delivering to customers and what our customers perceive.

Do You Know What Your Customers Really Think?

Most companies assume they're constantly giving customers what they want, but usually they're kidding themselves. Bain & Company surveyed

362 firms, and what they found was surprising: 80 percent of the companies stated they were delivering "superior experience" to their customers. However, when the customers of these companies were asked if they were actually delivering superior service, only 8 percent said yes. There's a massive gap between what most companies think they are delivering to their customers and what they are actually delivering. The best way to close that gap is to have a mechanism to gather ongoing customer feedback to inform how you improve your products and services.

Here's where it gets really interesting. More than 95 percent of management teams in the survey were convinced that their companies are customer focused. Despite this, Bain discovered that only 50 percent of these management teams tailor their products and services to the needs of customers, only 30 percent organize the functions of the company in ways that deliver superior customer experiences, and only 30 percent maintain effective feedback loops with their customers.[4]

T-Mobile's John Legere is a CEO who fully understands the immense power of feedback loops and obtaining information directly from the company's customers that is unfettered and unfiltered. Typically, when a new CEO is hired, he or she schedules lots of internal meetings, and everybody tells the new CEO what's happening in the company along with the key information they need to know. The new CEO may speak with a handful of customers who have tried and used their service, but very rarely do they ever understand what it's really like to be a customer of the company.

Legere discovered that the best way to get useful information is not to sit in rooms and listen to your people tell you what's wrong with the company. The best way to get actionable information is to ask your customers, putting yourself in their shoes to understand what's really happening. Then use that information to unlearn your worldview of your products and services and relearn what you should be building.

Legere didn't stop there. He sought to leverage technology to open up other customer feedback streams to unlearn even faster. In a *Harvard Business Review* article, Legere writes:

Much of what I do online is listen to customers, and social media is perfect for that. No filtering. If someone complains about T-Mobile, I'll tweet him or her my e-mail address and make sure we follow up internally.[5]

Legere gives an example of how an insight he gained from customer feedback resulted in relearning within T-Mobile's business strategy—and extraordinary breakthroughs and results. He learned that customers did not like the standard mobile phone industry practice of locking them into contracts and the extra fees (such as for roaming and data) that they neither understood nor had any control over.

Says Legere of his breakthrough, "It became clear that the best way to succeed in this industry was to do things as differently as possible from the existing carriers—to do the complete opposite. That was the start of the strategy we named Un-carrier."

T-Mobile's Un-carrier 1.0 plan—given the name Simple Choice—was contract-free and offered unlimited calls, unlimited text messaging, and 500 MB of unthrottled data each month for a flat rate of $50. Since Un-carrier 1.0 was introduced by the company in 2013, T-Mobile has rolled out numerous other customer-inspired Un-carrier strategies, including Un-carrier 5.0 (a free "test drive" of an Apple iPhone 5S for one week), Un-carrier 11.0 (rewards for T-Mobile customers, including free Subway sandwiches, Domino's pizzas, and much more), Un-carrier Next (a set of new rules to make pricing more transparent and other improvements), and more.

John Legere unlearned what he thought he knew about the mobile phone market, and relearned that the market was largely commoditized and the only way to get ahead was by exploiting competitors' weaknesses. He also relearned that people like authenticity from their leaders, not canned responses.

All this listening to customers led to breakthrough and a positive impact on T-Mobile's bottom line. In February 2018 the company announced that it signed on 5.7 million net new customers in 2017.

Total revenue for 2017 was up 8.3 percent over the previous year, to $40.6 billion, and net income for 2017 totaled $4.5 billion.[6]

Another reason T-Mobile powered ahead is that it totally owns the prepaid market. Legere discovered this breakthrough by simply listening in on customer phone calls and hearing the pain points the customers were having with contracts and fees—policies and procedures that they didn't understand which caused friction and made the purchasing process difficult for them. Unlearning that friction was the reason Legere and T-Mobile achieved such extraordinary results.

UNLEARNING PROMPTS

As a leader:

- How do you gather information against your vision, strategy, and product and services and how they are performing?
- What feedback streams do you have in place for both your external and internal customers? How effective are they?
- When is the last time the information you gathered offered new insight into how your product and services were performing or could be innovated? How intentional was it?
- How could you use the information you gather to inform your Cycle of Unlearning, and unlearn your customers' limiting company policies, practices, and strategies?

The Truth Is Out There—Are You Listening?

Another executive who actively seeks customer feedback—and then responds to it in near-real time—is Elon Musk, founder and CEO of Tesla, SpaceX, Solar City, and The Boring Company. Although there are many examples of Musk responding to messages directed to him on Twitter, this one is typical—and indicative of just how powerful feedback loops can be.

In December 2016, a customer tweeted a complaint to Elon Musk: "@elonmusk the San Mateo supercharger [public, high-speed charging stations available to Tesla owners] is always full with idiots who leave their tesla for hours even if already charged." Musk responded the same day with a tweet of his own: "You're right, this is becoming an issue. Supercharger spots are meant for charging, not parking. Will take action." Exactly six days later, Tesla put a new companywide policy in place:

> We designed the Supercharger network to enable a seamless, enjoyable road trip experience. Therefore, we understand that it can be frustrating to arrive at a station only to discover fully charged Tesla cars occupying all the spots. To create a better experience for all owners, we're introducing a fleet-wide idle fee that aims to increase Supercharger availability. . . . For every additional minute a car remains connected to the Supercharger, it will incur a $0.40 idle fee.[7]

A chief executive really doesn't get more responsive than that, using feedback received from a customer via social media to make a major, but quick adjustment in the company's international operations.

In another case, which occurred in September 2017, a *potential* customer tweeted a complaint to Musk: "@elonmusk had a terrible experience with very pushy sales guy from tesla Stanford shop while shopping for model x." Responding the very same day, Musk replied, "Def not ok. Just sent a reminder to Tesla stores that we just want people to look forward to their next visit. That's what really matters."[8]

Customer problems rarely change, but the technology you use to gather information (be it conversations, phone, social media, or data analytics platforms such as what Amazon, Facebook, and Google have created) changes all the time—enabling leaders to unlearn outdated beliefs and business strategies with faster and tighter feedback loops with real customers. The result? They relearn new behaviors, course correct, and break through to better quality products and services and increased customer satisfaction in new, innovative, and near-real-time ways.

What's particularly interesting is how both Legere and Musk personally engage, address, and resolve the problems their customers are facing. They acknowledge customers' issues and recognize that their products and services must constantly be innovated and improved, and the best source of information to inform that Cycle of Unlearning is from their customers. So they continually gather, actively solicit, and encourage feedback from customers. They make themselves vulnerable and open to direct feedback from their customers, yet strive for excellence in how they respond to that feedback. In return, the result is raw, unsanitized, and unfiltered information on how their products and services operate. That information becomes the input to their Cycle of Unlearning, enabling them to let go of past success and achieve extraordinary results.

It's everything that all of the traditional corporate operating mechanisms and executive behaviors are not. These leaders didn't delegate from their desks and create a hailstorm for their employees—another behavior to be unlearned. Instead, they took decisive action and addressed the issues directly. These leaders are continually unlearning what is not working, and then relearning how to improve to achieve continuous breakthroughs that enable them to leap ahead of their competition and accelerate away.

The Truth Is Out There—Go and See

Terminal 7 at JFK Airport in New York is operated by British Airways. The terminal was completed in 1970 and extensively renovated in 1991.

However, the terminal is showing its age, and British Airways decided that it was time to bring the facility into the 21st century. The leadership team also recognized that a new round of renovations would provide an opportunity to unlearn, shift their mindset and behavior as to how they do innovation, and co-create with customers while deeply involving them in the process.

We moved the executives out of their offices and set them up in one of the abandoned business lounges where we would map out and quickly test their ideas with real customers in the terminal. They could literally walk out of the business lounge and get feedback on their ideas in seconds. This was initially an extremely uncomfortable, unfamiliar, and unknown behavior for everyone on the leadership team. But they recognized—and soon realized—that to achieve their desired results they couldn't talk their way to unlearn; they had to take action to get there. What did these leaders discover?

New behaviors.

New ways of working.

New ways of innovating.

New ways of engaging stakeholders and customers to create more of what they want, and less of what they don't want.

By taking action and adopting these new behaviors, the team gained a new perspective, and in turn, a shift in their mindset. No more 100-page PowerPoint presentations in board meetings. Instead they created prototypes to provide real evidence of battle-tested ideas to show to the board, and new insights and information to inform better decision making and better investments, including a stop to creating products that customers didn't want.

The experience of going through the process and quickly testing their ideas with real customers was a powerful way for them to unlearn many of the beliefs they had about how the terminal was working and what customers wanted, and then relearn how to discover what in fact they really did want.

Seeing customers use their prototyped products and services, coupled with doing the testing themselves, enabled their breakthroughs to accelerate and compound. Creating quick and cheap prototypes, and testing them with customers, created safe-to-fail experiments for the executives to iterate the Cycle of Unlearning. They could then start to adapt their mindset, behaviors, and, ultimately, their products and services, to better serve their customers as they worked to extensively renovate and update the airport terminal.

Unlearn Sales, Relearn Service

Customers have always had problems with products and services, but they've never been able to talk directly to the CEO of the company that produced and delivered them. If they're lucky, they may get shuttled to a customer service rep halfway around the world. If they're unlucky, they'll get lost in your phone system, pushed from office to office until they finally end up in voicemail jail. CEOs like John Legere and Elon Musk recognize this, and they also realize it's a way to champion and demonstrate to their customers a better way to run a company.

This is fantastic marketing because nobody is telling you, "Oh, you should buy my product, it's awesome." Instead, you've got the CEO of the company literally at the end of the phone, tweet, or message that you're personally connecting with. And they're saying, "Thanks for your feedback. We are going to fix that. That's not the way we want our products and services to be delivered, and that's not the way we want our customers to be treated. You're helping us build a better product, so thank you again."

They're using technology to make a meaningful connection with their customers, co-create resolutions together, and adapt the policies of their entire business in days to new information and circumstances. They're unlearning the way that their products and services are operating and they're relearning—with the aid of their customers—to adapt those products and services and provide breakthroughs in the way that they're delivering them. This is profound in terms of the speed of the cycle, beginning with when a customer raises a problem, to when the leader recognizes the problem, and when the leader takes action by changing the system and making the company better.

Problems are always going to happen, but new behaviors and technology enable innovative ways to solve them. When customers reach out and they know they're being heard, and they know that their feedback is going to improve the product, they become more loyal to the product—and to the company. They become your ambassadors. They become your marketing team. They become the best sales team you'll ever have. No investment, no matter how great—even if you're spending in the neighborhood of $4 billion a year on marketing like AT&T—is going to be able to compete with customers who are so happy with your product that they are advocating actively on your behalf to their family, friends, and work colleagues.

Building Your System to Unlearn with Customers

When it comes to creating a system to unlearn with customers, these are the key questions I work through with leaders:

- How am I making decisions?
- Where am I getting that information?
- What's the quality of the information that I get?
- How frequently and quickly can I get it?
- How frequently and quickly can I respond to it?
- How is that information helping me to unlearn what's working and what's not with the products I'm building or the way my company is working?
- How can I use that information to relearn how we serve our customers?

- When I experiment and try different methods, how—and at what speed—will I discover whether or not they're working?
- How will I create situations that give me the breakthroughs to constantly improve my perspective of the world?
- How will I adapt my thinking and behavior to improve the way that I work and see the world?

Seeking Breakthroughs Is Your Responsibility

The problem with the legacy mindset and behavior of the executives who work on the twenty-first floor and never leave their offices is that people don't talk to them. They never understand what their customers are doing outside the company, never mind their internal customers—the employees of the business—and how they can help them succeed. Today's software and technology platforms are radically changing the way we discover new and interesting insights about our customers. And we can use that information to inform and adapt the way we behave.

What's most interesting to me about John Legere and Elon Musk is that they're using technology platforms such as Twitter and other social media to create tight feedback loops directly with their customers to unlearn. And when you think about the top five companies in the world that are powering ahead—Amazon, Facebook, Google, Microsoft, and Apple—what they're doing is building platforms that allow them to deeply understand how their customers are using their products and services. Based on the usage of all those platforms, they're able to unlearn a lot of the thinking and behaviors that are not working for them, and use that information to run experiments to help them relearn what will or won't work for their customers.

That means they progressively accomplish ongoing breakthroughs because they've built platforms to capture—faster, more frequently, and more accurately—how people are using their products and services to find out what works and what doesn't, and what they should be doing differently. That's why they're having exponential performance improvements relative to the rest of the companies in the Fortune 500.

Similarly, when you take that principle and apply it to an individual, that's where you see people, CEOs like John Legere and Elon Musk, having exponential unlearning experiences using existing technology platforms to connect directly with their customers, and use the information that they gather from those interactions to inform the products that they build and how to do it better, resulting in ongoing real-time breakthroughs. Because they make themselves accessible and vulnerable by putting themselves out there to be challenged, they inspire loyalty in their customers. And by responding to those challenges, they build better products and deliver better services that make their customers advocates for them.

A New Kind of Executive

The days of the CEO being a scary person, locked behind the door on the twenty-first floor, who had all the answers, are rapidly coming to a close. Information is democratized and free, and the people who have recognized that are the ones who are powering ahead. They're strong on their vision, but they're humble on the details about how to get there, and the way that they get those details is by soliciting and engaging their customers to help them bring their visions to life.

Leaders like John Legere and Elon Musk shortcut all the classical ways that leaders gather information about how their products and services are working—all the surveys, data, and reports—and go straight to the source. They're shortening the feedback loop, and they're iterating on the Cycle of Unlearning as frequently and effectively as possible. Their mindset and behaviors are radically different from those of most executives.

For years, leaders have tried to innovate the way they gather the information they need to effectively manage their organizations. Hewlett-

Packard popularized the most un-technological idea of "management by walking around" in the 1970s, where managers were expected to regularly get out of their offices and spend time with employees in their own offices and work areas. In the product innovation world, Silicon Valley legend Steve Blank talks about the importance of getting out of the building.

The answers to your questions aren't in your office; they're outside in the world, where people are using your products and services. If you really want to understand what's going on, you've got to go to the source, and you've got to be willing to listen. The popular television show "Undercover Boss" enables executives to ask the question, "What is it actually like to be a customer of your own business?" and then to experience the answer for themselves. In the show, executives go undercover in their own business—for example, taking a job as a cashier or warehouse worker—and find out the unvarnished truth about what's *really* going on in their organization. They're able to personally experience the gap and unlearn what they *think* is happening inside their business, and relearn what's *really* happening.

The people who power ahead are the ones who intentionally put themselves in that situation. It's uncomfortable; it makes them vulnerable. But the insights are worth it. They can use the information they gain to break their mental models and adapt the way that they work.

How you source and respond to the information your customers and colleagues share with you directly impacts the quality of what they share with you in the future, and the opportunities you will have to discover breakthroughs to higher performance, better products and services, and extraordinary results.

The Saga of the Ray Phone

From 1999 to 2017, Ray Davis served as president and CEO of Umpqua Holdings Corporation—the parent of Umpqua Bank, with headquarters in Portland, Oregon—and he still serves as executive chair of the company's board of directors. Since the beginning of his tenure with Umpqua, Davis proactively tried to find ways to distinguish his bank from the rest of a very large pack.

Visit an Umpqua branch (the company calls them "stores" not branches) anywhere in its fast-growing business empire, and you'll be greeted by a very different banking experience. The first Umpqua store is described on the company website:

> There was a computer cafe with free internet access . . . and our own custom blend of locally roasted coffee. We called this new location a store (not a branch) and opened it up to our community as a space they could call their own. Soon, customers and community members alike were hosting events in our store, and to this day you can find business meetings, book clubs, and even yoga classes happening inside your neighborhood Umpqua Bank.

But there was one more thing that made Umpqua banking stores different from any other bank or business you're likely to encounter. Inside every store, in a prominent location to make it easy for customers to find, is a phone with a direct line to the CEO's desk (Figure 8.1). When Ray was at his desk, he answered the calls himself. If he wasn't at his desk, and a caller left a message, Ray made a point of returning the call on the same day.

While decidedly not high tech, these telephones provide vital feedback from customers—unfettered and unfiltered by layers of management employees. Although Ray Davis no longer serves as CEO and so no longer answers the many Umpqua "Ray Phones" that he established in the bank's stores, his successor—CEO Cort O'Haver—has kept the tradition and now personally answers customer calls.

FIGURE 8.1.   The Ray Phone

PHOTO CREDIT: MICAH SOLOMON, MICAHSOLOMON.COM

9

Unlearning with People and Organizations

Our ability to open the future will depend not on how well we learn anymore but on how well we are able to unlearn.
—*Alan Kay*

On January 28, 1986, the space shuttle *Challenger*—one of five shuttles built by NASA—was set to lift off for its relatively short flight into orbit around the earth. The space shuttle program had been phenomenally successful, and *Challenger* had logged nine previous missions—taking its crew of seven astronauts into low-earth orbit to conduct experiments, deploy and service satellites, and gather scientific data. Previous *Challenger* missions had led to a number of firsts, including the first spacewalk during a space shuttle mission, the first American woman in space (Sally Ride), the first shuttle night launch, and more.

By the tenth *Challenger* mission, launches and landings—and the time in between, generally about a week—had become routine, even boring. Television networks used to interrupt their scheduled programming to cover Mercury, Gemini, and Apollo launches and landings, each of which pushed humanity's knowledge thresholds farther and had an undeniable edge of danger. However, after the first shuttle orbital test flight in 1981, the American public turned its attention elsewhere, and—except for a fledgling CNN—launches and landings were no longer broadcast live.

So when *Challenger* exploded and broke apart just 73 seconds after launch from Florida's Kennedy Space Center that cold winter morning—killing seven crew members in the process (including much-beloved school teacher Christa McAuliffe)—the event was a brutal reminder to the American people, and to the world, of the still very real dangers of space travel.

Just as had happened immediately after previous NASA catastrophic disasters—including Apollo 1 (where three astronauts were consumed by fire on the launch pad during a preflight test) and Apollo 13 (where a moon landing had to be aborted after the explosion of an onboard oxygen tank)—there were reviews and inquiries and commissions and self-assessments. The manned space program was put on hold until questions could be answered, practices examined, and systems improved, but most NASA veterans chalked up the *Challenger* disaster to a freak accident—an act of God that would not be repeated. In reality, engineers down the chain of command had warned against the launch, citing the low ambient temperatures, but their concerns were dismissed and overridden by managers up the chain. The explosion of *Challenger* touched a very deep nerve in the American people and in NASA's employees, and it was apparent that something had to change.

Breakthroughs or Breaking Points?

Throughout the late-1950s and early 1960s, NASA experienced a long series of remarkable technical breakthroughs in its human spaceflight program, culminating in the first moon landing in 1969 by the crew of Apollo 11. This tremendous surge in technology was in direct response to the challenge President Kennedy issued in 1961 to put a man on the moon by the end of the decade. Success followed success, as NASA moved from Project Mercury (which successfully put the first American, John Glenn, into orbit around the earth) to Project Gemini (orbiting with a larger spacecraft that accommodated two astronauts), and Project Apollo (with its three astronauts and lunar module, the vehicle that would take the astronauts to the surface of the moon and then back to the orbiting Apollo spacecraft).

But like any complex system or program that finds great success, it works—until suddenly, it doesn't. When work becomes routine and guards are let down, complacency sneaks in and performance suffers. That's exactly when the level of concern should be raised.

To succeed in the long run, organizations and the people within them must constantly be stimulated, and the capability of the organizational system of work continuously improved. In short, if the system appears not to be broken, that's all the more reason to fix it—*before* it becomes a problem and not after.

Indeed, as NASA was having tremendous success with its manned space program, the organization was sowing the seeds of failure, creating false intellectual superiority and impermeable towers of information. In time, these towers turned into silos, and they stopped information from moving across the organization. This became a very real problem for NASA, and it led directly to catastrophic failure with a resulting loss of life.

When your actions are achieving success, and moving in a positive direction, you gain more confidence to take greater risks. In the case of *Columbia*'s launch on January 16, 2003, the program managers were aware that heat-resistant foam tiles would routinely break loose from the surface of the shuttle's external fuel tank, but because they never had an issue with these errant tiles, it was a blind spot for them—they thought it was okay. They even gave it a technical term, "foam shedding," which served to further (as sociologist and professor at Columbia University Diane Vaughan defined) "normalize the deviance"* of this routine event within the shuttle team.[1]

---

* Vaughan defines this as a process where a clearly unsafe practice comes to be considered normal if it does not immediately cause a catastrophe: "a long incubation period [before a final disaster] with early warning signs that were either misinterpreted, ignored or missed completely."

That is, until 82 seconds after launch when one of the tiles, the size of a briefcase and 1.67 pounds in weight, broke loose and struck *Columbia*'s left wing—piercing the skin and causing internal damage that led the shuttle to break apart upon reentry into the atmosphere, killing all seven crew members. Video of the shuttle launch reviewed by NASA the next day clearly showed that the wing had been hit by a large chunk of foam.

Organizations of all sorts suffer from the normalization of deviance, until some catastrophe wakes everyone up. NASA employees turned a blind eye to ongoing deviations because the organization was able to complete its missions despite a few mishaps—until the universe hit back and catastrophic failure occurred.

In this chapter, we dig deep into unlearning with people and organizations, focusing particularly on a case study from NASA and the work it has done to learn lessons from some very pubic tragedies, while creating a culture of transparency and safety for mistakes, as they seek the breakthroughs required to build our future.

NASA Learns to Unlearn

A NASA veteran for three decades, Dr. Ed Hoffman served as chief knowledge officer of the agency (the first) for six years, until 2016. In this role, Ed was responsible for establishing a formal, integrated, and effective knowledge management program (with governance connected to NASA project management policy), a community of 15 formally assigned knowledge professionals, and a knowledge map of services and products. Ed is a mentor and collaborator of mine through our shared passion for learning and unlearning.

In his early years with the agency, Ed knew the importance of organizational learning, but the transformation was not an easy one for NASA. Says Ed:

The center point of what I've done in my career is this question: How do you get into a place where people are comfortable to take time to unlearn, to change what they're doing, to look at adaptive or different approaches, to innovate—and to move forward? I believe the biggest challenge with organizations is really the starting point of the comfort with unlearning. NASA was great at learning, but we usually had to fail really big before it became important enough for us to unlearn and then move forward.

It took catastrophic failure—the explosion of space shuttle *Columbia* in 2003—for the agency to get serious about unlearning its existing, dysfunctional learning culture. Previous disasters (including Apollo 1 and *Challenger*) were shocks to the collective consciousness of NASA, and people understood if different outcomes were to be achieved, they would need to take a different course of action.

The reality, however, was that many within NASA saw *Challenger* as a freak accident that would never again be repeated. They didn't think they needed to unlearn anything; NASA had a problem even using the word "unlearn" within the organization.

Key people in NASA struggled to unlearn the behaviors that had brought them so much success. They failed to let go of past success to innovate and build the future. On top of all that, after *Challenger*, NASA carried out a long string of missions without failure, doing what they had always done. This served as further evidence to many in the organization that *Challenger* was a freak accident, and the wise and prudent choice was to maintain the status quo, sticking with the behaviors that had always worked in the past.

Organizational transformation is the result of collective individual transformation; it is continuous, not a one-time event. As such, it must be active, adaptive, and ongoing. We must continuously seek to unlearn the behaviors and thinking that are holding us back, then relearn and apply new methods to achieve the breakthroughs that lead to extraordinary results. Waiting for failure events to prompt action is the definition of failure to unlearn and innovate your organization's system of learning.

Learning organizations are not only about transforming workers, a common misconception on the part of many leaders. Leaders *and* workers must both transform together. To achieve organizational or systemic impact, leaders and trainees must be trained together and act in sync with one another. In a post-*Challenger* NASA, this was definitely not the case.

But all this changed after the *Columbia* disaster. Even those who believed that *Challenger* was a one-time act of God realized that NASA's problems were systemic and had to be addressed by everyone in the organization—together. So Ed applied the same problem-solving approaches that the agency performed in space on the ground. He worked within NASA to build systems of learning to inform decision making, doing the research and interviewing people across the entire organization to better understand what behaviors led to success and what behaviors led to failure. He encouraged people to share their stories with his knowledge team—and with one another. Mistakes and mishaps were occurring regularly, but they were not openly talked about. Smart people like to be correct—they are used to being correct. Talking about failure wasn't a cultural or behavioral norm at NASA.

Ed and his team built a new system of learning based on the inputs they gathered from every corner of the organization, at every level. This system identified competencies and then trained people, giving them the tools and opportunities they needed to use new behaviors.

After *Challenger*, NASA struggled as leaders found it difficult to unlearn the behaviors that made them successful. But eventually, they began to understand what they needed to unlearn and relearn to achieve the breakthroughs they wanted. After *Columbia*, NASA's leaders were trained and given authority, and they deployed the new system to full effect. When employees came to senior leaders with ideas for change, the leaders would tell them, "Go out there and do it." This led to the development of new written policies and guidelines—written *by* employees *for* employees, which led to better outcomes, including these two specific ones.

The first one was alignment and engagement. When initial policies were drawn up and distributed to the workforce, the natural reaction was to be skeptical and reject the changes: "They don't do projects in Washington, what do they know about my work?" When policy, procedures, and standards were set from a community of experienced practitioners, the whole dialogue shifted. NASA unlearned to centralize policy creation and relearned to have experienced practitioners from the field draft all standards and policies, given that they have the validity of practice. It also helps engagement because the community will protect its own. Ed and the practitioners did this by making sure that the larger community has access to communication, conversation, and input. A policy may not be optimal (it rarely is in initial drafts), but it has the wisdom of the knowledge community impacted.

The second outcome involved learning and competencies. Once NASA had practitioners developing policies, Ed and his team could bring them into the NASA Academy as teachers to train and communicate the competencies. This is vital because when you are being taught by a valued practitioner, it raises the value. For example, NASA was having significant problems with orbital debris. (Space junk is a massive problem.) Ed could not find industry or academic expertise to design a course, so he worked with a NASA and international expert on orbital debris and they together designed a course for aerospace professionals. The course then became the basis for policy. This was not unusual. Often a starting point would be to learn about the problem, prepare learning materials that would be presented to students at NASA, listen and collect their feedback, unlearn what was not working with the course, and then redesign a stronger one.

The Key Components to Relearn Systems of Learning

Creating continuous organizational transformation can be quite a challenge, but as was ultimately the case for NASA, it can be done—and done well—but you must design for it. When working with clients, designing and deploying their system of learning is the key to scaling sustainable learning and unlearning throughout their organization. The small steps I use to get started are as follow:

- First, understand the system by gathering data and interviewing people from across the organization, at all levels.
- Identify the competencies that lead to successful outcomes, and those that do not.
- Design a system of work that allows the desired behaviors to happen, and socialize it with your community for communication, conversation, and input.
- Think big but start small. Don't try to deploy all the new behaviors at once. Identify the one you feel can have the most impact and start there.
- Make the new behavior really easy to do, then provide a small group of people with new tools and training in the new behaviors.
- Give people designed opportunities to deliberately practice new behaviors but start small, such as sharing information with one another (good and bad) to show evidence, and quickly make them feel successful using the new behaviors, thus reducing learning anxiety and increasing psychological safety.
- The system in design needs to be tested by the people who will use it (its customers) during and throughout the design process. Once you have designed, tested, and deployed the new system, get more and more people to use it and generate results. Take the results and use them to improve your system as you scale.
- Constantly stimulate the system of learning so organizational complacency and intellectual arrogance does not take hold. Give people designed, safe-to-fail opportunities to remind them of what happens when failures occur, such as simulated system failures or exercises (piquing survival anxiety).
- Eventually, the organization gets to the point where the new system becomes widely adopted, and the organization and the people

in it start recognizing what it needs to learn and what it needs to unlearn.

When working with global organizations to transform, I constantly have to remind leaders that scaling yourself does not work; scaling your lessons learned does. People remember stories and take inspiration from the experiences of others. Start by encouraging peers, colleagues, and teams to share their experiences, discoveries, and difficulties based on specific behaviors, methods, or mindsets they have tried to unlearn. By making it easier for everyone to learn from one another, you leverage the company's collective information and insight. This builds momentum, creates new norms, and enables your organization and the people in it to achieve extraordinary results.

Google's Aristotle project revealed that creating great teams wasn't about how smart or how experienced people were. Instead, it was how much psychological safety resided within the group.[2] Having a safe space for team members to share mistakes and be vulnerable in front of one another was the number-one indicator of high-performance teams. When mistakes are seen as new information available to improve the system, not negative information to show an individual's inabilities, it can become a competitive advantage for your people and your organization.

Creating a culture of sharing lessons learned and reducing learning anxiety helps to grow an organization's capability. The more safety there is, the better the quality of information, the better the quality of decisions, and the better the quality of results. This is the basis of a performance-oriented, generative culture outlined by Ron Westrum.

So how did NASA's decision makers unlearn being the "know it all" and transform into being the "learn from all"? The first small step and new behavior NASA implemented was sharing stories of success and failure. Ed Hoffman and I use the Pyramid of Advantage or Catastrophe model to help people understand why making, catching, and sharing mistakes is a good behavior. It prevents mishaps, which in turn mitigates catastrophic failures.

As a leader, your responsibility is to enable organizational learning by reducing learning anxiety across the entire organization. The purpose of a learning organization is to help others make *better* mistakes, not the *same* mistakes.

Ed Hoffman talks about three levels of uncertainty that impact the desired outcomes of missions (Figure 9.1): mistakes, mishaps, and catastrophic failures. According to Ed, a *mistake* is when something doesn't go according to plan; a *mishap* is when the mission or project doesn't fail, but some part of it is going in the wrong direction; and a *catastrophic failure* is when things have not gone right, resulting in significant negative consequences. Each situation offers the opportunity to learn, and NASA's new system of learning trained employees to raise and discuss mistakes when they occur—in a safe space without judgment—so they don't become mishaps or catastrophic failures (Figure 9.2).

Harvard Business School professor Chris Argyris once pointed out, "Smart people don't learn . . . because they have too much invested in

FIGURE 9.1. The Pyramid of Advantage or Catastrophe

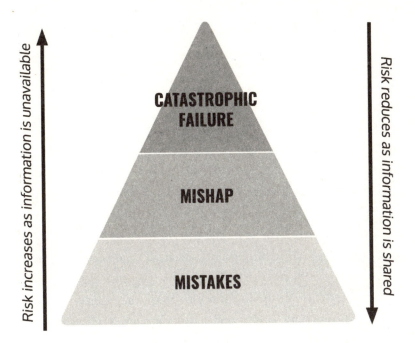

Risk increases as information is unavailable

Risk reduces as information is shared

CATASTROPHIC FAILURE

MISHAP

MISTAKES

FIGURE 9.2. The Pyramid of Advantage or Catastrophe risk and information flow

proving what they know and avoiding being seen as not knowing." Without safety, smart people struggle to reveal their shortcomings; NASA was faced with a similar challenge. The organization had lots of smart people, but they didn't have a smart system of learning, sharing mistakes, or unlearning. The key is to make people aware of the consequences of not sharing mistakes, and then to normalize sharing mistakes as a learning opportunity or even a competitive advantage.

Future Breakthroughs Require Relearning from the Past

When you do true innovation, you're never guaranteed successful outcomes all the time. Failure is inherent because you don't know what you don't know. So you need to build learning systems that surface mistakes before they have a chance to become mishaps or catastrophic failures. This requires instilling a behavioral norm of sharing mistakes and using the information to improve the system. Psychological safety is the key metric for high-performance teams.

When you truly innovate, build the future, and courageously face down uncertainty, what happens is that complex, unpredictable, and unintended consequences occur. When you build hierarchies of knowledge or silos, and information doesn't travel across the company, organizational learning does not occur. You need to unlearn this approach to information management, and then encourage a culture of making safe-to-fail mistakes and socializing those mistakes (and successes), because it feeds into this knowledge pool that lifts the entire capability of the company. You're trying to institutionalize the kind of behaviors in which people are constantly sharing and promoting and learning from what they're doing, what's working, what's not working, and democratizing information because it becomes a powerful capability, a source of most current knowledge, and a competitive advantage for the company.

Unlearning Deviant Behavior

One of the big problems that NASA (and many other organizations) had to overcome was the normalization of deviance that was discussed earlier. It is when you're in a situation and you've defined organizationally or as a team what behavior indicates successful performance. When a deviation to that comes up, where behavior is not happening correctly or the way you expect it to—but that deviation doesn't lead to a failure—then the deviation becomes normalized, routine, and acceptable, even if such behavior is not ideal.

This can happen when you're very busy, overloaded with tasks, or when complacency creeps into the system. You don't have a lot of investment and resources. You don't have time to reflect. You're too tired to explore every deviation in performance. You enlarge the margins of acceptable behavior, and you therefore start normalizing and accepting deviant behavior.

At least two systemic problems led directly to the explosion of *Columbia*. First, NASA's program managers ignored the ongoing problem of heat shield tiles falling off the launch vehicle and hitting the surface of the spacecraft. This occurrence was within the acceptable limits for a shuttle launch since it had not led to any significant consequences in prior missions besides a few dents. It became a tacitly accepted—*normalized*—deviance. Second, NASA program managers became overconfident even when mishaps (foam shedding during liftoff) were occurring routinely. They were blind to the possibility of catastrophic failure.

Normalization of deviance occurs in every kind of organization, not just a government agency like NASA. For instance, there are many types of normalization of deviance, especially behavioral aspects of people in companies. Uber and former CEO Travis Kalanick are prime examples. People started raising concerns about his ability as a leader several years before the company's toxic culture was exposed and he had to step down, but the company was growing like crazy, so Kalanick's behavior was overlooked by many. There's a natural tendency for some organizations and leaders to say, "It didn't fail. It didn't blow up," so it becomes normalized and acceptable—until it impacts the organization with consequences that may have serious repercussions.

To illustrate how NASA's learning organization changed for the better after the *Columbia* disaster, Ed tells the story he calls, "The Tale of Two Shuttles." The first shuttle was *Columbia*, and the second shuttle was *Discovery*. Both encountered problems, handled largely with the same people in the room, but in a totally different way. When the decision was made by *Columbia's* program managers to launch despite the possibility of a tile strike to the wing, the result was a catastrophic disaster. The *Discovery* launch took place six years later. Ed Hoffman flew to the Kennedy Space Center in Florida to witness the launch. But all did not go according to plan. Says Ed:

I got down there that night and everything was looking good. I woke up the next morning and grabbed breakfast at about 6:00 A.M. It was then that I was told we might have a problem. The problem was that at the end of the last shuttle mission, which landed successfully, there was a small but significant technical issue where one of the flight control valves did not operate properly. There were four of these valves with plenty of redundancy, so it wasn't a problem. The shuttle landed safely. But the engineers could not explain why the valve did not operate properly. Was it something in the process? Was it a part from a supplier? They couldn't explain it.

We were in exactly the same situation as we were with *Columbia*. Something had deviated. On initial viewing you don't think it's something that's going to be a problem. What do you do?

In those shuttle meetings there were as many as 200 people in a room, including senior leadership, the astronaut crew, engineering, safety, retirees—the whole community. The problem with the valve was raised, and a launch decision needed to be made. The program team recommended a launch. They said, "We can't explain why that valve is a problem, but we've flown successfully. We have these other valves that are working well." There are heavy costs when you sit on the pad and don't launch. Not launching also increased the risk to the International Space Station, which was counting on the shuttle's arrival for supplies. But engineering and safety said *Discovery* shouldn't launch for the simple reason that they couldn't explain what happened and they should figure that out first.

Following the *Challenger* disaster, Ed worked within NASA to create a program management initiative, which later became the NASA Academy. Workers were trained, given leadership and innovation tools, and provided with learning opportunities to relearn new approaches to old problems and deliberately practice new behaviors. But when these men and women went back to their departments, they were told to ease up by their leaders, who held onto the behavior norms they attributed to success from the past, and still saw *Challenger* as a freak incident.

Following *Columbia*, the breakthrough NASA realized was that adopting new behavior norms required that both leaders and workers change together—progress could not happen in isolation. If NASA was to create the cultural transformation they desired, and continuously adapt their systems of learning, training programs, and behavioral norms individually and collectively, leaders and workers had to unlearn, relearn, and break through together.

Discovery was originally scheduled to launch in January 2009, but this date was pushed back until the team could solve the problem with the control valves. The team's leadership focused on the key outcome of assessing the acceptable risk to launch, sourcing input from multiple groups closest to the problem while managing the organizational tensions of available information, safety, budget limitations, and dependencies such as the astronauts on the space station who were anxiously awaiting a fresh supply shipment.

NASA made the decision to invest in experiments to resolve the issues, eventually creating a new, patented technology that allowed testing without putting the shuttle in danger. This required many extra hours and greater costs but led to an innovation that created a more resilient shuttle that would be less expensive to test in the future. The team solved the problem with the valves and successfully launched *Discovery* in March 2009. Says Ed about the decision to delay the launch:

> That was one of the days I was most proud of being part of NASA and whatever contribution I made to the organization because, during that day, there was total learning taking place. We had most of the same exact people working both missions— *Columbia*, which went in a completely wrong direction—and *Discovery*, where the approach and the dynamics lent themselves to learning. If organizations and projects follow that kind of an

approach consistently, the success rate for everything they do would skyrocket.

Ed's story clearly illustrates NASA's breakthrough resulting in an improved system of learning and organizational behaviors in operation. The leadership team exhibited that they had unlearned normalization of deviance and relearned cross-functional collaboration, multiple disciplinary input, and transparent sharing of information, while managing the tension of acceptable risk in decision making for launch. NASA did this by:

- Raising and making transparent the mishap with the shuttle valves
- Involving everyone affected by the decision
- Focusing on what really mattered
- Balancing financial and safety tensions with the mission's desired outcome
- Leveraging organizational insight
- Making a decision and everyone committing to it

The result was further successful missions after a mishap, new innovations in shuttle testing, and the control valve problem being solved. The decision was made by the team to stop, make a fixed investment in exploring the problem, and avoid failure. They balanced the competing risks, resulting in a stronger system of learning and better organizational behaviors overall, and a safer and less expensive shuttle.

Unlearn Complacency and Arrogance to Scale Your Breakthroughs

Every organization runs the risk of backsliding into its previous state, falling victim to complacency as the next disaster looms just around the corner. One way to prevent this from happening is to revitalize the system of learning by piquing survival anxiety, so people remember that failures can and do happen, especially in unguarded moments.

As we have seen, NASA is definitely no stranger to catastrophes, but it has been many years since the last catastrophic failure: space shuttle *Columbia* in 2003. Without the occasional significant failure every three or five years to refocus everyone's attention on what can happen when complacency sneaks back into the system, disaster awaits. To prevent this, you have to train, reflect on results, and have conversations that remind people what happens when things go bad. You have to be curious enough to introduce new behaviors into existing routines. Remember: Individual and organizational transformation is not a singular event. It is continuous, and we must constantly stimulate the system to discover and exhibit new and better behaviors. This is the purpose of deliberate practice of the Cycle of Unlearning.

To help its employees remember, each year NASA conducts what it calls a Day of Remembrance. On this very special day, NASA pauses "to reflect on the legacy and memory of our colleagues who have lost their lives advancing the frontiers of exploration." In his message to employees for the 2017 Day of Remembrance, NASA's acting administrator, Robert Lightfoot, pointed out that approximately 45 percent of the current NASA workforce were not working for the agency 14 years earlier, at the time of the *Columbia* tragedy. Continued Lightfoot,

> How do those of us who experienced tragedies and subsequent recoveries ensure the lessons are passed on as we continue our exploration journey? The best way I know is for us to share our stories—not in PowerPoint—but personally.[3]

During the Day of Remembrance—the last Thursday of January each year—the families of astronauts who died in the Apollo 1, *Challenger*, and *Columbia* tragedies are invited to speak about their loved ones, and employees who were there at the time are encouraged to share their own stories. They are also invited to share their personal stories about the accidents—and the return to flight efforts—in team meetings during the month. Explained Robert Lightfoot, "Perhaps then all of our team will begin to understand the reason we strive for a culture of speaking up with concerns, and a culture of leaders who stay curious and hungry as they make the ultimate decisions to send our crews on their journeys."[4]

Some of today's most successful companies have learned similar lessons, although the impact of their decisions are not life and death, as they can be for NASA. For example, Netflix has found that it can effectively leverage deviant behavior to improve their systems of organizational learning, as well as products and services. The company conducts game days where, unbeknownst to the teams, parts of the company's live production systems are randomly shut down and their products and services start breaking. The purpose of the exercise is to build a system that can identify and mitigate failure, be more resilient, and improve the quality of their system of work. Intentionally disabling computers in Netflix's production environment also builds alignment and collaboration networks among employees across the company, ultimately enabling them to provide their customers with a better quality of service.

No one on the Netflix teams would know why suddenly their products and services were breaking and whether it was real or not, but the exercise trained people to actively collaborate and share the information they had with one another to find and fix the failures, thereby building greater resilience into their systems. Intentionally disabling computers in Netflix's production environment became such a habit within the company that they built a piece of software called Chaos Monkey to randomly and automatically trigger system failures to test how their systems and teams responded to outages. Chaos Monkey is now part of a larger suite of tools called Simian Army, which was designed to simulate and test responses to various system failures, edge cases, and outages. In addition to leveraging deviant behavior to improve their systems, these simulations help Netflix people constantly introduce new approaches, ideas, and paradigms on a steady basis to continuously improve their systems of learning, products, and services.

Unlearning does not lead with words; it leads with action. By unlearning the ways in which we behave, our actions begin to change the way we observe, experience, and eventually see the world. Seeing and experiencing the world differently changes the way we think about the world. People do not change their mental model of the world by speaking about it; they need to experience the change to believe, see, and feel it.

Innovation, such as new behavioral norms, also need a petri dish in which to grow. It requires a protected and safe space for people to start to unlearn old skills and relearn new ones. Safety needs to exist at many levels, including psychological, physical, and economic. We need a sandbox in which to experiment, and to test and develop new skills, capabilities, and mindsets. We must design and create an environment where we can make recoverable mistakes without causing irreversible damage.

Sandboxes create the safety we need to get comfortable with being outside our comfort zone to innovate and succeed. Physical sandboxes create dedicated time and space to allow our new behaviors to emerge through trial and reflection. Economic sandboxes allow us to make safe-to-fail investments to relearn, acquire new skills and capabilities, and deal with uncertainty without blowing up the entire business.

As you increase the level of safety in your organization, check the reactions and responses of your people when failure occurs in the team. Do they act as though they are beaten, or is the new information seen as a competitive advantage, leveraged, and fed forward to the next iteration? High-performance generative cultures see incidents as competitive advantages.

The Power of Continuous Unlearning

In a company setting, adopting the Cycle of Unlearning requires that we unlearn the belief that identifying, designing, and deploying systems of learning are a one-time event. As organizations from NASA to Netflix to Toyota have proven, where systems of continuous learning are implemented, simulated, evolved (sometimes automated, such as with Netflix), and made a part of the cultural norm, you can achieve extraordinary results.

Taiichi Ohno, the father of the Toyota Production System, famously stated, "We are doomed to failure without a daily destruction of our various preconceptions." He knew that success for Toyota required employees to unlearn, let go of the past, and seek new, innovative, and powerful improvements each and every day. Toyota understands that to build its future, one has to be ready to unlearn, adapt, and apply new methods as the world continuously evolves.

As BJ Fogg's Tiny Habits teach us, adopting new behaviors is not as complicated as people believe. Even more, it is a system. Unlearning leads to more unlearning and can become systemic with ripple and network effects across your entire organization. We simply need to decide what we want to unlearn, make deliberate choices, and introduce new behaviors to existing routines. When NASA innovated its new learning system after the *Columbia* disaster, leaders and workers learned and engaged in new behaviors of cross-functional collaboration. They shared mistakes and lessons learned, and they used this knowledge to make better decisions.

Relying on motivation alone to bring about change will not work. We need to make it easy to do, regardless of an individual's ability. We must also start with small steps, integrating them into our existing daily routines to slowly but surely commence the journey to see and experience the world in new ways. This can be as small and easy to do as asking others in your organization what the most helpful mistake is that they recently made. How did it help them make a new discovery to improve what they were working on? By iteratively working on small, frequent steps—adapting our approach based on what we discover—we build momentum and evidence of evolution based on the results.

How to Start the Cycle of Unlearning and Become a Learning Organization

The simple truth as stated by Andrew Clay Shafer, senior director of technology at Pivotal, is, "You're either building a learning organization, or you're losing to someone who is." That premise is very pertinent in today's world. The idea of a learning organization is nothing new. As I explained in Chapter 2, the idea was popularized by Peter Senge in his book *The Fifth Discipline*, which was published in 1990.

The reason NASA, Netflix, and other true learning organizations succeed is that they have a systematic approach to taking in information from all sources of their organization, synthesizing, leveraging, and then using it as the basis upon which to innovate. They actively create opportunities and safe environments for people to learn by doing through experience, informal settings, simulations, and play.

Informal, incidental learning takes place wherever people have the need, motivation, and opportunity. After a review of several studies done on informal learning in the workplace, Victoria Marsick and Marie Volpe concluded that informal learning can be characterized as follows:

- It is integrated with daily routines.
- It is triggered by an internal or external jolt.
- It is not highly conscious.
- It is haphazard and influenced by chance (something sparks).
- It is an inductive process of reflection and action.
- It is linked to learning of others.[5]

So, what are the components of a learning organization, and how can you measure if yours is one? Victoria Marsick and Karen Watkins developed a model of a learning organization that comprises seven different parts, as well as the Dimensions of the Learning Organization Questionnaire, or DLOQ, to diagnose an organization's current status (Table 9.1).[6]

DIMENSION	MEANING	DEFINITION
Continuous learning (1)	Create continuous learning opportunities.	Learning is designed into work so that people can learn on the job; opportunities are provided for ongoing education and growth.
Inquiry and dialogue (2)	Promote inquiry and dialogue.	People gain productive reasoning skills to express their views and the capacity to listen and inquire into the views of others; the culture is changed to support questioning, feedback, and experimentation.
Team learning (3)	Encourage collaboration and team learning.	Work is designed to use groups to access different modes of thinking; groups are expected to learn together and work together; collaboration is valued by the culture and rewarded.
Embedded systems (4)	Create systems to capture and share learning.	Both high- and low-technology systems to share learning are created and integrated with work; access is provided; systems are maintained.
Empowerment (5)	Empower people toward a collective vision.	People are involved in setting, owning, and implementing a joint vision; responsibility is distributed close to decision making so that people are motivated to learn toward what they are held accountable to do.
Systems connection (6)	Connect the organization to its environment.	People are helped to see the effect of their work on the entire enterprise; people scan the environment and use information to adjust work practices; the organization is linked to its communities.
Strategic leadership (7)	Provide strategic leadership for learning.	Leaders model, champion, and support learning: Leadership uses learning strategically for business results.

TABLE 9.1.   The Seven Dimensions of Organizational Learning

What's particularly interesting about this model is that all these constituent parts of organizational learning can be seen in action within some of today's most successful companies. For example, Amazon builds systems specifically designed to capture learning and use it as they measure their teams. In this book, we talked about the ideas of feedback, reflection, experimentation, and synthesizing what you've learned. In essence, this is the breakthrough step in the Cycle of Unlearning—it all ties together.

The first version of DLOQ comprised 43 descriptive statements divided across the seven dimensions of organizational learning, but this was later reduced by Marsick and Watkins to 21 questions. Here are examples of some of the descriptive statements from the most recent DLOQ:

- Q1. In my organization, people help each other learn.
- Q2. In my organization, people are given time to support learning.
- Q3. In my organization, people are rewarded for learning.
- Q4. In my organization, people give open and honest feedback to each other.
- Q5. In my organization, whenever people state their view, they also ask what others think.[7]

I encourage you to consider working through this questionnaire with your own organization, starting with yourself and your team. Identify the dimensions in which you are lagging—maybe it's continuous learning or empowerment. Pick one dimension, discuss, decide, and commit to one thing you believe your team must unlearn to move forward. Write an unlearn statement for it, and then design a tiny habit to unlearn it; make it really small. Think what you could do in a month, in a week, or in a day. Introduce a new and better behavior to take its place.

As you work through the Cycle of Unlearning, design and build a system of organizational learning. For example, NASA's approach to identifying key competencies of success, then training employees, giving them tools, and creating opportunities for them to practice these competencies.

Scale the learning system across your entire organization and normalize desired behaviors—while removing deviant behaviors—the same way Ed Hoffman did at NASA. Make the learning system your default condition, not something used only when management is looking.

Finally, systematize your learning system. This is what technology companies do by default. They build learning platforms to gather data to inform their decision making. It is here where you will reap the full benefit of the learning organization by routinely unlearning old behaviors that no longer work and replacing them with new behaviors that will enable you to achieve extraordinary results.

10

Unlearning Incentives

The iron rule of nature is: You get what you reward for.
—Charlie Munger

I can vividly remember the day not that long ago when I had the opportunity to sit in on an executive strategy team meeting of one of the world's largest banks. I was invited to give my perspective on the necessary conditions for creating high-performing organizations, specifically the required leadership mindset and behaviors, and compare and contrast it with what the bank was doing. The meeting ran two hours, but the first 90 minutes or so were devoted to the attendees trying to outdo one another in terms of how well their businesses were performing, and the exceptional figures they were getting—evidenced by their perfect records and positive indicators of success.

There was a shift during the last 30 minutes of the meeting, however, when the attendees started to discuss topics of interest to the company as a whole—specifically, what was the bank's purpose, where they should go in the future, and how they could improve the ways in which they worked together.

The room went quiet for a minute, and then the person responsible for the largest individual component of the bank spoke up. "Basically," the executive said, "we're designed as a business to compete against one another, and the side effect of this design is that we don't share information with one another. We constantly look for opportunities to improve our individual businesses instead of working together to improve the overall performance of the bank."

It was true. This high-power team of executives would never be able to move the entire organization in the direction they wanted if they kept optimizing just for themselves. To be even more successful as an organization, these executives would need to stop doing what had brought them individual success in the past and start doing what would bring the bank success in the future.

While that's all well and good, the realization and admission on the part of the executive leadership team was illuminating. It brings us to the heart of a question that would determine their ultimate success: What are the incentives driving these financial executives to change the way they work and their own behavior?

The big question (and challenge) for executives is what motivates and enables them to take the risk, to innovate, or to unlearn what has brought them success in the past? Most executives are measured on very specific business outputs and financial metrics, and if they can demonstrate a percentage point more effectiveness or more efficiency, they're guaranteed to get their big bonus payouts. If that's the case (and it often is), then why would any executive take a course of action that is uncertain, risky, or unknown—even if the payoff was 25 percent or greater effectiveness or efficiency?

In this situation, what would *you* do?

Leaders in most organizations today are massively incentivized to do what they've always done and squeeze a little bit more out of the existing system, versus taking a risk and unlearning what has delivered past success. When you pair up this reality with how executives are conditioned to compete with one another, which doesn't foster collaboration across the organization, this leads to a tremendous gap between potential performance and the performance that is actually experienced in organizations.

I'm reminded of what former General Electric CEO Jack Welch

once said: "Any jerk can have short-term earnings. You squeeze, squeeze, squeeze, and the company sinks five years later."[1] The incentives in most organizations favor short-termism, local optimization, and what's easy to measure—practices that work against long-term success. In this chapter, I concentrate on unlearning incentives by exploring how to move the focus from individual outputs that benefit just a limited number of people or departments, to system-level outcomes that benefit the entire organization.

Incentives and Unlearning

How do people let go of what has made them successful in the past to find extraordinary results in the future? One of the reasons people get trapped doing the same things they've always done is because of organizational incentives that drive their behaviors. These incentives are often financial in nature, including pay raises and bonuses. Research shows, however, that relying on pay for performance may actually drive negative behaviors and disincentivize people from modifying what they do.[2]

Consider the example of a CEO and other executives who run a company. A significant portion—likely the majority—of the executives' incentive structure is based on the performance of the company. If the stock price goes up or profitability increases, executives will get big bonuses. So immediately, their minds go straight to their bonuses and not on doing what is necessary to create an exceptional company or a great place to work.

If you create a contingent relationship with your employees based on rewards by saying, "If you do *this*, you will get *that*," then they will have a natural tendency to focus on the "get *that*" part of the equation. If, for example, you tell managers that they will get a bonus for reducing operating costs, then the managers will put their full focus on taking costs out of the system, perhaps even to the detriment of the overall organization and its long-term growth prospects. And as the magnitude of the "get that" increases—as bonuses rise into the tens and hundreds of thousands of dollars—then executives and other employees will do whatever it takes to earn them.

Research shows that the percentage of company payrolls dedicated to bonuses versus pay raises has increased considerably since 1991, when 5 percent of company payrolls was devoted to raises and 3.1 percent to bonuses. As of 2017, this figure had increased to just 2.9 percent of company payrolls devoted to raises, and 12.7 percent to bonuses.[3] However, these figures don't reveal the full extent of the problem with bonuses and the contingent relationships companies create with their top executives. According to an article in Fortune, 90 percent of CEOs' total pay is composed of performance bonuses, including long-term incentive pay—leaving just 10 percent to CEOs' salary. As of 2014, the median of these CEO bonus payouts was $7.1 million—up 6 percent from the year before.[4] Median CEO pay for the 100 largest companies reached a record $15.7 million in 2017.[5]

With this much at stake, which outcomes will CEOs naturally put their greatest focus on? The risky ones that could jeopardize their bonuses, or the status quo of past success they are certain will guarantee they will "get *that*"? What would *you* do?

When the stakes and rewards are this high, leaders are faced with two options: Do I stick with what's known that has brought me results in the past, and then squeeze the system to get the 1 or 2 percent more that I need to guarantee my bonus? Or do I be courageous, embrace uncertainty, and unlearn? Do I do something different that I've never done before with the potential upside of extraordinary results—or the potential downside of massive failure? Inevitably, 99 times out of 100, they choose to stick with what they've always done. Indeed, the companies these men and women work for get what they reward.

Existing incentive structures are one of the biggest inhibitors for driving innovation in any organization. Leaders think they've designed them to lead innovation in the company, but they actually have the reverse effect. They provide rewards at the individual level while extracting systemic-level costs.

It's time to unlearn individual pay-for-performance incentives and relearn to create the conditions for authentic motivation, courageous behaviors, and exploring risky initiatives in a controlled manner to get the breakthroughs to achieve extraordinary results. The strategy is that you don't suddenly change everything you're doing and work in a new way. Think big but start small. Pick one or two initiatives in your portfolio that you can experiment with in a safe-to-fail manner. Instead of betting the farm, you're placing a $1 bet on a new way of recognizing people and their contributions. When you start to see the benefits of those small experiments, that evidence will encourage you to take on more audacious experiments, uncertainty, and risks.

Breakthroughs Happen When You Align Effort to Outcomes

Another problem leaders often encounter is measuring the output of individuals without tying their performance to—and making visible their contribution toward—the system-level outcome. Leaders need to define a system-level outcome, a purpose, and a mission that people can believe in, clearly understand, and are motivated to achieve. Then they must ensure that individuals can see alignment with what they want to achieve, their contribution, and the system-level outcomes they are impacting.

Providing clarity of system-level outcomes, helping people get started, and then providing support along the way is the responsibility of leadership. All too often, companies aren't clear about what the purpose of the business is or the mission to achieve, and employees aren't clear how their contribution ties to either.

At Netflix, the key role of leadership was to make sure everybody clearly understood what were the top priorities of the organization at any given time. They then encouraged people to do what they believed would be most effective in achieving those very clear objectives that the entire company was working toward.

In her book *Powerful: Building a Culture of Freedom and Accountability*, Patty McCord—who served as the chief talent officer at Netflix—explains that her litmus test was being able to stop any of the company's employees, at any level of the company, in a break room or elevator and ask them this question: "What are the five most important things the company's working on for the next six months?" If they couldn't reel them off one, two, three, four, five, ideally using the same words used in communications to the staff, then Patty knew that Netflix leadership was failing to do its job, not the individual.

If people don't understand or are not clear on the intent of the company, they can never move toward it. And if you don't incentivize people to achieve the intent and measure that as success, then they will optimize for other objectives, the easy-to-measure incentives that are attainable to them but not necessarily the intent of the company.

The majority of people are measured on their activity, not what they contribute to system-level outcomes. This occurs because individual activities are much easier to measure. Companies and managers often claim that it's too hard to measure system-level outcomes, so they don't—or they communicate them poorly while failing to ensure the alignment of work to these system-level outcomes. The result is that people become disengaged from their work; they can't see the outcomes they are affecting. They lack clarity about what they're trying to achieve so everyone just does what they need to do to guarantee the "get *that*" side of the contingent equation—the outputs that are easiest to measure for which they will be rewarded. Leaders must unlearn that hard-to-measure outcomes are rarely achieved by completing only easy-to-measure tasks.

People want to have a sense of contributing to the greater good—of their organizations, their communities, and the world at large. Employees are most satisfied in their work when there is a strong link between what they do and compelling system-level outcomes they're contributing toward. When the link is weak or absent, then motivation and performance are sure to suffer.

UNLEARNING PROMPTS

When managers communicate what they will measure, it sends a signal to people what behavior the company considers to be important and will monitor to evaluate their rewards. Take a moment to consider the initiative you are currently working on.

- What metrics do you monitor?
- What signals do the metrics you monitor send to teams?
- Are they easy or hard to measure?
- Are they system- or local-level outcomes?
- How can you tie your effort to the system-level outcomes the project is aiming to achieve?
- If you improved all the easy-to-measure tasks, what impact would this have on your system-level outcomes?

The Science of Incentives

One of the grand challenges of leaders everywhere is: How do you motivate people to do what *you* want them to do—especially if it is something *they* don't wish to do? As you know from Behavior Design, everyone is different, and different behaviors motivate different people in different, often unintended ways.

It's evident there is a fundamental disconnect and behavior matching problem within organizations. According to the 2017 Gallup State of the Workplace report, 85 percent of employees globally are either actively disengaged (18 percent) or not engaged (67 percent) at work. Says Gallup, "This latter group makes up the majority of the workforce—they are not your worst performers, but they are indifferent to your organization. They give you their time, but not their best effort nor their best ideas.

They likely come to work wanting to make a difference—but nobody has ever asked them to use their strengths to make the organization better."

What is the result from all this lack of employee engagement in their work? A whopping $7 trillion in lost productivity globally.[6] While a lack of engagement doesn't explain the entirety of employee motivation issues (one can be engaged but not want to do something because one disagrees with it), I believe there is a connection.

In 2016, MIT economist Bengt Holmström (along with Oliver Hart) received the Nobel Prize in Economics Sciences for his work in the field of contract theory, including addressing the "principal-agent" problem, which according to the *Financial Times* is "the problem of motivating one party (the agent) to act on behalf of another (the principal)."[7] There are a variety of relationships where this problem can occur, including relationships between employees and managers, CEOs and shareholders, patients and doctors, and so forth (Figure 10.1).

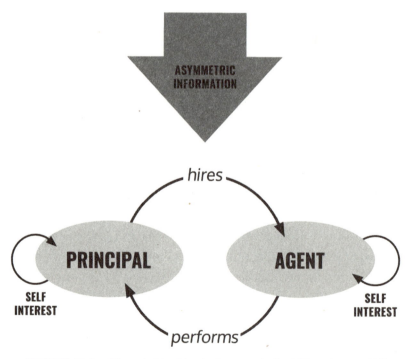

FIGURE 10.1. The relationships between principal (P) and agent (A)[8]

As part of his work on contract theory, Holmström aimed to study, experience, and observe how the principal-agent model, the prevailing approach to incentives, *thinks*. His first discovery was that the model makes too many inferences based on the principal's viewpoint of the agent's performance. It asks, "How much does this performance show that the agent did what the principal wanted them to do?" The problem being that the principal rarely, if at all, sees what the agent actually does. If employees have a successful outcome, for example, then their manager believes they worked hard to achieve the desired outcome. If, however, employees have unsuccessful outcomes, then their manager believes that they didn't work hard to achieve the desired outcome—they must not have been motivated or had the desire to succeed. The reality is many factors can impact outcomes. Customers might not want the product you created, an unexpected issue may arise, or you can be unlucky with timing.

People also don't just produce effort. The work they do is multidimensional, and the time devoted to quality versus quantity of output ultimately determines performance. How people are incentivized determines in great part where they will focus their effort. But people struggle with measures that aren't well aligned with the entire package of what is being incentivized, and they struggle with assessing hard-to-measure tasks.

Holmström identified and cautioned that when tasks get complex you shouldn't zero in on one incentive. When people do, they focus on what's easy to measure and not on what is hard to measure—which typically happens to be the desired outcome. We must incentivize hard-to-measure tasks that lead to desired system-level outcomes, *not* easy-to-measure tasks.

Attempts to improve performance by linking it to pay will not result in the desired outcomes. This leads to poor results, yet this is the prevailing approach in most organizations—an approach that has existed since the Industrial Era when managers walked around measuring outputs of work with their checklists, ticking the boxes for what each employee was doing. Many leaders today continue to hold on to this Industrial Era conditioning and mindset, which needs to be unlearned.

Consider the recent Wells Fargo scandal that resulted from employees being rewarded by the company for creating up to 3.5 million bogus accounts.[9] The system-level outcome Wells Fargo was aiming for was better customer satisfaction and increased usage of their products and services. What's one easy-to-measure indicator of that? The number of new accounts opened. The more accounts opened, the better the customer satisfaction must be, or so Wells Fargo's executives thought.

The initiative was at first successful; but, when Wells Fargo employees ran out of real customers to open new accounts, they created fictitious customers and were rewarded by the company for it. That is, until this practice was revealed to the public.

When you optimize locally, create strong incentives based on pay for performance, and measure only the behaviors that are easy to measure, the focus turns toward the individual employee's activity, not the system-level outcomes. You end up with unintended consequences and deviant behavior. In the case of Wells Fargo, the company paired an easy-to-measure "if this" (the number of new accounts) with bonuses (the "get that") meant to increase productivity output. These bonuses caused employees to focus on the rewards, resulting in unintended consequences and greater risk, brand damage, and $185 million in fines.[10]

In his research, Holmström recommended when unlearning the principal-agent model for incentives and relearning a new system, consider the following questions.

"What if there were no incentives?" In cases where employees have clarity of purpose in their work, alignment on how their efforts contribute to achieving it and appreciation for their efforts are enough to prompt the desired behaviors.

"What if there needs to be an incentive?" When incentives are required to motivate an employee to work harder or perform a less satisfying or undesirable task, modest financial incentives such as a small bonus can have a significant effect. But not all incentives must be financial: You can offer personal development, career paths, family flexibility, and other nonfinancial rewards.

Holmström's winning thesis framed how pay for performance doesn't solve the incentive problem but *is* the problem. And the key first step to remedying the problem is a mix of easy-to-measure tasks along with hard-to-measure ones.

Relearning What People Really Want

Employees want to be appreciated, and companies actually have many instruments to make people feel appreciated and motivate them in their work, beginning with job design. 3M famously encouraged its technical employees to spend 15 percent of their time pursuing their own ideas, a remarkably progressive program that started in 1947. This practice resulted in a variety of product innovations for the company, including Post-it® Notes. Companies can provide career advancement opportunities, allow employees to work from home, offer open time off, and much more.

When incentives are done right, people feel appreciated and engaged in their work. When done wrong, employees put in the minimum amount of effort to get the most out of the incentive system. This only leads to negative outcomes for all parties and incentive theater.

A few years ago, researchers for employee engagement firm TINYpulse conducted a survey of more than 200,000 employees working for more than 500 organizations. Among other items, the survey asked respondents this question: "What motivates you to excel and go the extra mile at your organization?" The survey provided 10 possible answers, which rank as follows:

- Camaraderie, peer motivation (20 percent)
- Intrinsic desire to do a good job (17 percent)
- Feeling encouraged and recognized (13 percent)
- Having a real impact (10 percent)
- Growing professionally (8 percent)

- Meeting client/customer needs (8 percent)
- Money and benefits (7 percent)
- Positive supervisor/senior management (4 percent)
- Believing in the company/product (4 percent)
- Other (9 percent)[11]

As you can see, money and benefits ranked well below peer motivation, feeling encouraged and recognized, having a real impact, and professional growth.

Transforming Talent and Incentives at Capital One

Drew Firment is the former technology director of cloud engineering at Capital One and the current managing partner at A Cloud Guru. In his position at Capital One, Drew worked with executives and teams from each of Capital One's distinct business groups across the enterprise—including card, retail, and commercial banking—on cloud adoption and talent transformation. Drew learned firsthand the power of incentives and creating systems that encourage employees to give their best by appreciating the outcomes of their efforts.

Capital One wanted to achieve a number of system-level outcomes, including faster delivery, less expensive operations, and increased product innovation. The company realized that these outcomes would best be achieved by utilizing the cloud. It was a strategic priority for founder and CEO, Richard Fairbank. Said Richard, "Increasingly, we're focusing on cloud computing and building the underlying capabilities such that product development will be faster and more effective over time."

For the cloud adoption program, the organizational strategy was to migrate Capital One's systems from on-premises data centers to the public cloud as quickly as possible, in a manner that was well-architected, secure, and cost-efficient.

To make this happen, it would be necessary to translate the organization's strategy to divisional objectives, then align with department plans, and finally drive individuals to the right actions and behaviors. It was critical to establish intent and a common answer to "Why does this matter?" and "What's the opportunity for me?" for all parties.

When organizations want to achieve breakthroughs, they must first define the system-level outcomes the company is trying to achieve. Then they must communicate them clearly, ensure people understand them, and measure them (even if they are hard to measure). It's vital to connect people's individual efforts to the system-level outcomes they are aiming to achieve and show how they are contributing to them. The same is true with adopting new behaviors.

Drew points out that Capital One is loaded with ambitious Type A personalities and has a culture geared toward high performers and high achievers. But like that of many large enterprises, its performance management system was a barrier. With an annual review process tied directly to compensation, individuals were incentivized for the short term. Says Drew:

> Although what really needs doing is things that are the long-term, hard-to-measure, system-level outcomes—a team is generally incentivized for what they're going to deliver within the performance management cycle. When your compensation is tied to short-term objectives, you end up delivering short-term outcomes.

Drew knew that a focus on the short-term, easy-to-measure activities wasn't going to lead to the long-term, system-level outcomes Capital One's CEO identified: increasing the speed and effectiveness of product delivery to customers. This would require moving Capital One to the cloud and lead to another set of outcomes: improving the speed, quality, and cost of cloud migrations with an eye on the underlying individual talent transformation that fuels Capital One's innovation.

Relearning the Definition of Success

During a pivotal leadership meeting, Drew was inspired to take action. It didn't make sense to use an abstract maturity model to measure organizational performance and cloud adoption. Instead, the leadership team should be specific about what success looked like—based on three key outcomes set by Capital One's CIO—and then measure it using the underlying audit trails available in the cloud. Even if it turned out to be hard to measure, they needed to be aligned to system-level success. It might not be perfect, but it would create a shared understanding of purpose, and where the organization and the people within it stood with regard to achieving their mission. According to Drew, the best system would provide:

> a very clear destination, understanding your current position with real-time data, and directions that are consumable. You provide visibility with a dashboard and instrumentation that allow individuals and teams to self-assess if they're on track or in need of repair. This helps to align individual efforts to organizational outcomes.

Drew was convinced that reframing measures of success would provide the breakthrough Capital One needed. The past behavior of applying abstracted maturity models had to be unlearned, and the group needed to relearn to focus on defining their own specific, hard-to-measure, system-level outcomes to achieve the extraordinary results they desired. Drew partnered with a developer and created the Cloudometer (Figure 10.2). This system measured the metrics that mattered—the speed, quality, and cost of cloud migrations—and individual talent transformation.

Then came the harder part: figuring out how you incentivize the *who* to do the *how* to get to the *what* and *why*.

Some approaches worked, while others did not.

On the "what worked" side of the equation, Drew realized that to

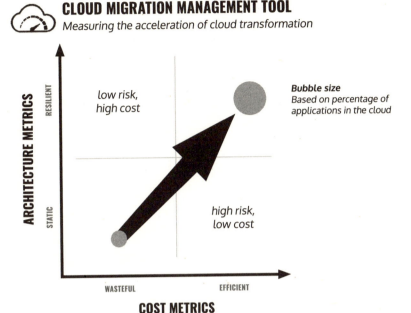

FIGURE 10.2.   The Cloudometer

achieve the strategic objectives, a massive transformation of cloud computing skills would be necessary. Providing individuals with a career path for achieving a valuable, industry-recognized cloud certification offered a professional growth incentive, while also enabling people with the skills to achieve their department objectives. Remember BJ Fogg's tactics to create new behaviors? Give people training, new tools, and resources, or make the new behavior really easy to do. Then make them feel successful as quickly as possible as they exhibit the new behaviors.

Drew created a Cloud of Fame where the names of employees who earned their certifications were publicly displayed for all to see. It became a badge of honor for those who earned a place on it—they knew their contributions were recognized and appreciated by the organization—while gamifying the process of personal development and healthy cross-company competition. In addition, when employees earned their certifications, Drew sent an e-mail message to his or her manager, that manager's manager, and *that* manager's manager—three levels up. Individuals' efforts to learn cloud computing were reinforced as valuable, creating positive peer pressure for others to participate and contribute.

While divisional-level certifications were inherently a vanity metric and easy to measure, it created a very visible information radiator for sharing the competency levels of teams, and provided a leading indicator for the rate of training uptake of individuals adopting the skills required to achieve the desired system-level outcomes. Correlating and mixing the easy-to-measure increased competency levels with improvements in system-level, hard-to-measure key performance indicators (KPIs) visualized in the Cloudometer reinforced the value of supporting individuals in their personal journeys. As individuals earned their certifications, providing visible recognition of their accomplishments was also important to success. Each small achievement—or tiny step—helped people feel successful and appreciated as they worked to realize greater system-level outcomes.

On the "what didn't work" side of the equation, for a few departments supporting legacy maturity models, their hardened culture was too strong to influence. Those managers who held onto their individual, localized status-quo metrics didn't move. This layer of frozen middle management was a strong barrier between their staff and the disruptive strategies threatening the status quo. People do what their managers reward. If they reward output, that's all you'll get. If they reward contributions toward system-level outcomes, then people will focus on that. Remember: The KPIs you communicate to the team—what you make visible and signal you're looking at to employees—will lead to the behavior you get.

Most of the individuals within these departments recognized the opportunities presented by a shift to cloud computing. Even so, they inevitably prioritized actions that would be valued and rewarded by those in control of their end-of-year ratings and financial incentives, not the bank's system-level success.

Safety and Transparency

Drew recognized the need to align organizational or system-level incentives to achieve Capital One's desired outcomes, and he worked within the company to do this. Capital One is a metrics-driven company, and KPIs are used to highlight the misalignment of team-level activities and adoption of new practices with organizational outcomes. But success would ultimately be found in moving all the departments from only easy-to-measure metrics to a mix of easy- and hard-to-measure metrics, from vanity metrics to actionable ones, and from science fiction to harsh facts. But transparency is a double-edged sword. Says Drew:

> In my experience, slow adoption in the early phases of transformation is usually masked by internal marketing and wishful bias. The early phases of Agile in enterprises is a great example—many teams faked Agile by implementing meaningless ceremonies while reciting the manifesto. Real transformation occurred once organizations shifted from useless vanity metrics (for example, the number of story points or tasks completed) and focused on outcome-based metrics (for example, percentage increase in customer satisfaction or reducing time to market).

Similar to Agile adoption, cloud transformation was initially slow, and masked by the enthusiasm within the echo chamber of early pioneers. Establishing a visible set of key performance indicators in the Cloud-ometer created visibility into the slow rate of adoption. The outcome-based measurements were critical to triggering the need to better align system-level incentives with outcomes. The visible display of outcome-based metrics was very uncomfortable for many departments since it exposed their gaps in skills and execution. In a culture that is incentivized based on a distribution curve, that information could be misused for political and personal gain when comparing individual and team performance during end-of-year calibrations.

If it's not safe to share the negative information and use it to improve the system, then people won't risk the exposure. People will share only the positive information—the information that won't get them in trouble—or game it to get their reward. As a result, improvements are based on poor quality of information, and thus the system never really gets smarter. It's theater. Drew was fortunate to work with leaders who provided him the air cover and psychological safety to share the correct information which revealed the gaps but enabled them to be addressed—the positive effect of negative information. This was vital to success.

Breakthroughs Create Positive Unintended Consequences

With individual actions aligned to visible system-level outcomes, a new behavior emerged in Capital One with *learning communities*. Individuals began to work in cooperative groups to learn cloud computing, which created opportunities for community leaders to pay it forward by facilitating sessions and helping peers on their own personal transformation journey.

Unlike past technologies that had a much longer shelf life, cloud computing was evolving rapidly with constant releases of new features from Amazon Web Services (AWS). The old training methods (such as instructor-led training) couldn't scale or keep pace. The organization had to unlearn how to learn and shift to a continuous learning paradigm that relied on self-sustaining and empowered learning communities—as Ed Hoffman did at NASA.

Capital One encouraged people to build knowledge in cloud computing starting with AWS certifications. They didn't support a fixed mindset of, "Good, you've got your certification. You're done." They championed a growth mindset of "Great achievement! How can you apply it and help others?" They were encouraged to better themselves and their teams, and that's what people were recognized for, not just for completing a specific activity or certification.

As a company, Capital One realized innovating its technology systems required talent transformation. "We have a strategic imperative for a pretty dramatic transformation of our technology capabilities as a company. And this is a transition from being a company with an IT organization or an IT shop to really being a technology-led company. The hardest part of that transition is really a talent transformation," said Rob Alexander, CIO of Capital One.

Unlearning Incentives in Your Organization

When designing incentives, remember Charlie Munger's words: "You get what you reward for." Identify your desired system-level outcomes, then make visible and clearly signal to employees what behavior you are looking for. If you change KPIs, that impacts behavior. Financial incentives can be effective—as can a variety of nonmonetary incentives. If you decide to go the financial route, keep in mind that a small bonus can have a great effect.

The problem I saw with individual incentives such as in the large bank mentioned at the beginning of this chapter is that it created lots of negative competition among people in the organization, which led to them actively trying to trip up one another. While the system worked for the individual, the organization suffered in the long term because people were optimizing for what was good for them, and rarely optimizing for what the company was trying to accomplish.

The executive leadership recognized the need to unlearn, and we worked together to relearn their definitions of success, switching individual activity to shared system-level outcomes. We mixed easy- and hard-to-measure KPIs that people could clearly align their effort as contributing toward, resulting in greater clarity for teams, collaboration between departments, and significant returns for the organization.

Achieving system-level outcomes requires creating an environment of psychological safety for people to work within. Transparency in how information is treated is key to creating such an environment and to the ultimate success of the organization.

Capital One's Cloud Center of Excellence (CCoE) designed and operated a massive talent transformation program that increased cloud fluency throughout the organization. More than 15 percent (and counting) of the technology group has earned AWS certifications, enabling the organization to reach beyond the tipping point of critical mass toward a sustainable transition to the new operating model. One of the key ways of measuring success was tracking the number of AWS certifications and correlating the impact on migrations using the Cloudometer management tool to visualize, measure, and demonstrate how training contributed toward achieving the desired system-level outcomes the CEO had defined (Figure 10.3).

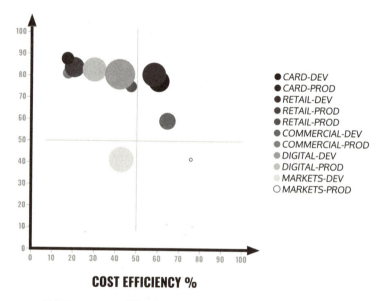

COST EFFICIENCY %

FIGURE 10.3. The Cloudometer system-level outcomes

Today, Capital One, the tenth largest bank in the United States, has the highest percentage of virtualized infrastructure of any major bank in the country, all residing in the cloud. They had an amazing transition, and Drew helped drive the talent transformation with an innovative approach that intersected strategy, engineering, and education at scale.

11

Unlearning with Business and Product Innovation

I can't understand why people are frightened
of new ideas. I'm frightened of the old ones.
—John Cage

As with business and product innovation, unlearning also requires constraints to challenge us to think and act differently. The NHS National Programme for IT (NPfIT) in the United Kingdom is the most expensive software project failure in history, costing £12.4 billion before it was scrapped in 2011 (the original budget was £2.3 billion). Members of Parliament described NPfIT as "the worst and most expensive contracting fiasco" ever. (In fact, some officials have claimed that the final cost was as high as £20 billion since commencing in 2002.)

The NPfIT was intended to transform healthcare services in the United Kingdom, digitalizing patient records, connecting 30,000 general practitioners to 300 hospitals, and providing secure and audited access to these records by authorized health professionals. The program was dogged with problems from the outset. The NPfIT had a big vision and a big budget. They thought big, built big, and it became too big to fail. A multitude of suppliers, including Accenture, Fujitsu, British Telecom, and CSC, signed on to deliver the program, but when challenges struck, they all pointed fingers at one another instead of figuring out how they could work together to overcome them. Some suppliers eventually terminated their contracts, making them liable for huge sums of money for withdrawing from their projects. Yet, few of these penalties were ever recovered.

Following such a negative run of results, a small group of 30 people took an alternative approach that saved time and money. They learned to unlearn many of the behaviors and accepted thinking to seed the beginning of a radically different outcome with extraordinary results. They thought big but started small to make a systemic and lasting impact on how governments should and would deliver IT projects for years to come.

The path to these outcomes wasn't an easy one. Not only did the team have to unlearn many of the prevailing behaviors, governance procedures, and methodologies that supposedly reduced risk and provided predictability of successful delivery, they also had to help the United Kingdom government and its civil servants unlearn outmoded information and outdated behaviors, and then relearn new and counterintuitive approaches to innovation. But that they did. They achieved numerous breakthroughs and extraordinary results in the most bureaucratic and regulated environment known to humans: government institutions.

It wasn't by any means straightforward. But led by Andrew Meyer, a small team showed that the Cycle of Unlearning can work in the most difficult domains; in fact, it excels in them.

Rebuilding the National Spine

The National Spine—the electronic backbone of Britain's National Health Service—is an IT infrastructure service originally developed as part of the troubled NPfIT and operated for the benefit of all NHS organizations throughout the United Kingdom. It joins together more than 23,000 healthcare IT systems in 20,500 separate organizations,[1] connecting everyone from physicians to administrators to records keepers to researchers to patients themselves. The system is comprised of three main components:

- **The Personal Demographics Service (PDS).** This is a cradle-to-grave record containing detailed information on every patient that follows them throughout their entire life.
- **Summary Care Record (SCR).** This provides a summary of each patient's medications, allergies, and adverse reactions.
- **Secondary Uses Service (SUS).** This supports the payment of £30 billion to hospitals in the United Kingdom. It also supports the planning of NHS services and research, providing access to anonymized patient record data to create business reports and statistics for research, planning, and health delivery.

In addition to these three main components, Spine also has a messaging function to support communication among all the different participating organizations and individuals and an identity and access management service. Users can insert a smart card into their PC or laptop, enter a PIN number, and, depending on their role in the system, gain access to information on Spine.

British Telecom (BT) had been running the notoriously fragile service for the 10 years since its inception and was coming to the end of its contract. Andrew Meyer and his team had lived through the NHS National Programme for IT, and they thought there must be a better way to approach the necessary upgrades and improvements to Spine. The timing was propitious as the UK government—burned by the previous, multibillion-pound overrun and failure of NPfIT, and armed with the extraordinarily high quotes of £1 billion to redevelop the Spine system—was looking for new approaches that didn't hand over so much control to large private corporations. In addition, the government's emerging Information and Communications Technology (ICT) strategy, which defined system-level outcomes for large information technology projects, put the kibosh on contracts over £100 million and emphasized the use of agile techniques and open-source technologies.

So, instead of contracting out the work, Andrew Meyer decided to try to unlearn the mistakes of the past and do the work in-house. Spine 2 was born and with it a new approach within government to product innovation. According to Andrew, this was a huge pivot in strategy and behavior for the organization, a tremendous difference from where they were. Says Andrew:

> We were an organization that was for all intents and purposes an assurance organization. We went around with clipboards and checked that other people did things the way we thought they should be doing it, as defined in our requirements and contracts. If something went wrong, we would pick up the phone and say, "Something's gone wrong. It's not working as specified. You must fix it for us."

Ultimately, there were three major aspects of the organization's behavior and mindset that needed to be unlearned to initiate the Cycle of Unlearning that Andrew's organization required to completely transform how work was done within it.

The first major shift was taking the work away from contractors and moving it in-house. While contractors had clearly not performed well in previous NPfIT projects, there was no guarantee that the government IT team would do any better.

The second major shift involved moving away from proprietary, off-the-shelf tools provided by Oracle and other industry behemoths, to open-source technologies. This approach introduced the possibility of jettisoning whatever stability and limited success the original Spine platform had gained and opening Spine 2 up to greater potential failure.

The third major shift was using a more iterative and adaptive approach to delivery instead of the big up-front design, release, and stage-gated methodology employed throughout governmental institutions. While a better outcome relative to the NPfIT initiative was virtually guaranteed, it would require a wholesale transformation in the culture within Andrew's IT group and governmental organization.

All the unknowns made people in the organization extremely nervous, and Andrew had a very challenging time getting people to buy into the fact that the organization needed to let go of the past and unlearn to succeed. Getting past this hurdle required Andrew and his team to be courageous while facing tremendous uncertainty. Ultimately, the organization achieved extraordinary results, delivering a robust Spine 2 system that worked reliably while responding to the growing needs of its many stakeholder groups. But this individual and institutional transformation required a great deal of unlearning, and then relearning, to break through.

Think BIG, But Start Small to Safely Transform Yourself, Your Teams, and Your Organization

To begin the Cycle of Unlearning, Andrew's purposeful, cross-functional team of 30 had to behave quite differently than it had in the past. For example, an IT contract with a large budget must go through a lengthy, internal business case and funding process which could take 18 to 24 months to get fully approved. By the time the sign-off finally occurs, there's tremendous pressure to complete development within fixed time, budget, and scope constraints—sometimes in just a few months.

Getting around this obstacle required unlearning the old, bureaucratic system that governed large, high-cost projects, and relearning a new approach that would result in much faster, safer, and smaller steps to achieve the team's desired outcomes. Says Andrew:

I broke the business case up into smaller chunks, which allowed me to ask for smaller amounts of money. That approach allowed us to crack on with development and exploratory work associated with the redevelopment of the Spine 2 service. When you have a big project, you need big budget, which results in a big business case that takes a long time to work through the review and approval process. We came to the realization that if we could leverage the existing system's natural constraints, it might be more effective to think big but start small.

Andrew and his team unlearned their long-held approach to doing work and getting projects approved in big batches. They relearned that by working in small batches, it was easier to understand the work, complete it end to end, and get feedback more quickly from real users of the system. It also had the added benefit of creating a safe-to-fail work environment as no batch of work ever became too big to fail. It became simpler to scope, fast to fund, and relatively cheap to learn what worked and what did not. Each delivery increment created new information to guide next steps and demonstrated that a new way of working could deliver extraordinary results. The small steps also served to create momentum and validated that their new behaviors were achieving the intended outcomes, helping the team members to feel successful as quickly as possible. They worked within the system to unlearn the system, relearn a new one, and then break through.

By dividing the work into small business cases, Andrew and his team were able to fly under the radar to a certain extent: The projects weren't so large that they would get the attention of senior civil servants and administrators. But Andrew's innovative approach didn't stay under the radar for long. Eventually, a very senior civil servant asked Andrew what he thought he was doing and gave him quite an upbraiding. During their tense exchange, Andrew responded to the bureaucrat, "I did that because that was what was needed to do to deliver this project." His approach was working, and the civil servant couldn't deny that.

Andrew asked the government official if he wanted him to stop what he was doing, and the bureaucrat responded simply, "No, don't be silly. I don't want you to stop—but don't do it again." This was a standard Industrial Era management mindset: You disobeyed—don't do it again (but I'll take the results).

This response is really no surprise from a long-serving official in a deeply bureaucratic culture such as the NHS. Even though there was clear evidence that the old system was broken and the team's new approach was working, the first response was to reprimand Andrew for not following the status quo. Instead of asking, "You're getting extraordinary results. How did you do it?" or "What can we do to help others adopt your approach?" the response was, "Don't do it again."

Breakthroughs Require Courage, Not Comfort

The easy road is to revert to old behavior and comfort when you are in the trough of uncertainty. When you're in front of people who are putting pressure on you and your team and banging on the table, saying, "Why are you doing something different?!" remind yourself what prompted you to take that courageous first step, and unlearn. Brené Brown once said, "The middle is messy, but it's also where the magic happens." When you're in the messy middle of the Cycle of Unlearning—as you are relearning new behaviors and methods, challenging the existing paradigm, and beginning to feel it might be too hard—that's actually when you need to channel courage and accelerate your efforts to get the breakthrough you need.

There's also deep institutional unlearning that Andrew—and anyone who dares to take an alternative path within organizations—must deal with. The majority of management teams are naturally fearful of supporting or sponsoring a new approach that may or may not work. Managers wonder what's in it for them. If they green-light a new initiative, it could fail and take them, their rewards, and their careers down with it. The potential downside is too great. This is but another reason to start small, be safe to fail, and demonstrate the effectiveness of how new behaviors can succeed before scaling. Your small steps are the evidence that creates the confidence to secure their support.

Interestingly enough, when Andrew and his team flipped the product development model on its head by making the decision to build in-house, the team was suddenly seen as a supplier—an outsider—and the rest of the organization wanted to assure what *they* were doing. Andrew explained that he wanted the other parts of the organization to be part of the solution, not walking around with clipboards and checking whether they had completed their work correctly. By saying this, Andrew was trying to help the rest of the organization unlearn its governance approach by way of cross-functional collaboration instead of contract negotiation.

According to Andrew, when he was much younger, he was quick to jump to conclusions, telling everyone: "This is absolutely the way to do it." Matthew May, author of *Winning the Brain Game: Fixing the 7 Fatal Flaws of Thinking*, calls this cognition behavioral pattern *leaping* to solutions without first clarifying or framing the problem you're trying to solve. The manager's instinctive reflex is, "This is how I've always done it—I was successful as a result, and I'll continue to be successful by doing what I've always done." But this is a shortsighted way of thinking and behaving. The conditions of the world constantly evolve, as does the situation in which the manager may have solved a similar problem in the past. In addition, there are new technologies, new ways to experiment and learn, and new ways to innovate how things are done.

To relearn and break through, the organization and its leadership must first unlearn:

- Requiring employees and teams to follow a status-quo process even though it's broken, not longer fit for purpose, and doesn't produce the desired outcomes
- Punishing employees when they independently take ownership of a problem and solve it

- Causing employees to work under the radar to change the system from within due to lack of support from the top

In short, the organization's negative results are due to the bad systems of work that the leadership team has designed, implemented, and is responsible for. Leaders must relearn to co-create systems with their employees (they're customers) that work for all. When they do, the breakthroughs and performance improvements are exponential and potentially endless.

Starting Small to Relearn with Customers

NHS has about 1.2 million employees—that is, customers to serve—and each has different requirements, wants, and needs. There was no way that Andrew and his team could serve all 1.2 million users at the outset of the Spine 2 effort, so they scaled back their focus to a subset of users—about 10,000—and their key needs (there were over 1,000 requirements in the team's original backlog).

As the team worked on the project, it became clear that they weren't going to be able to deliver on schedule. So they worked with a targeted subset of users to identify what they thought were the most critical features that would make the service usable from day one, and then they focused on creating those. Other features would not be delivered on day one but would come over time.

The first unlearning is that you don't actually need the majority of what customers tell you they want. Instead, relearn to co-create and collaborate with customers to deliver what they really need, together. Focus on a small set of needs and deliver them quickly and frequently to your targeted set of users. As they provide feedback on what they need next, respond. Work on that next set and deliver it to them in small, fast, and frequent batches. And so on.

To this day, Andrew's team has not delivered all the functionality the original business case promised because users realized they don't actually need the majority of what they believed they wanted. By relearning that software products and services can be delivered in small batches of work quickly and continuously after the first and each subsequent release, the behavior of the users of the system starts to change. Users saw evidence that they were getting the functionality they needed, as well as the improvements that resulted from the feedback they provided to the Spine 2 team.

Most companies need to unlearn how they engage their users and customers. Instead of waiting to engage them at the end of the process, they need to engage them early, often, and throughout the entire life of the product or service. Delivery is only complete when the system is sunset or retired, not when it is first released. When you adopt these behaviors and mindsets, you get tremendously valuable feedback from your customers and you can focus on building the features they actually need. Iterate and improve them, based on feedback from real users, in much the same way as Elon Musk and John Legere do with the products and services they deliver.

The Unlearning Organization

To unlearn is incredibly difficult because everything you know is the sum total of your experiences throughout your lifetime. Everything you learn is also not unquestionably good. You can learn the wrong lessons, bad habits, and flawed ideas. Unlearning bad behaviors is harder than learning them in the first place.

The key to find the best results for your situation is to introduce very small, easy-to-do, and safe-to-fail new behaviors that provide people with evidence of something working in a different way, making them feel successful with the new behavior, and enabling them to see progress toward the outcomes or aspiration they wish to achieve. Once they start to experience this new world, they build confidence in it. People cannot think their way to unlearn; they need to take action to relearn and behave in a new way to get the breakthroughs to achieve the extraordinary results they desire.

Remember, Turn Obstacles into Opportunities

Many people assert that there are "special circumstances" and differences between them and global innovators and business disruptors such as Google, Amazon, or Netflix that are held up as examples of product development "done right." I often hear, "We're unique" and "That won't work here." That may be true, but people often look in the wrong places for the obstacles that prevent them from reaching for extraordinary results. Detractors will treat size, regulation, perceived complexity, legacy technology, or some other special characteristic of the domain in which they operate as a barrier to transformation. While these obstacles are indeed challenges, the most serious barriers are found in organizational culture, leadership, and strategy—all of which can be affected by thinking big but starting small to unlearn outdated, legacy behaviors, to relearn better behaviors, and to break through.

A highly regulated and extremely bureaucratic environment is challenging and impacts the effectiveness of people who are used to working in a more collaborative way. But as with any customer, engaging regulators earlier and more frequently can help them see evidence of good governance through the delivery of real working products instead of ticking boxes and checking lists. Stellar outcomes can be had with a small group of dedicated people who are focused on a challenge and funded by a modest investment.

In the case of Andrew and his team, instead of users not finding out what the software would look like for a year as they did under the old behaviors, the Spine 2 system showcased what they would deliver even before the team started to build it. Users had input on the design process. Instead of asking the bureaucrats to fund a multibillion-pound initiative,

Andrew broke down the initiatives into tiny chunks with a much smaller and faster funding cycle—none more than £100,000.

The strategies that Andrew and his team deployed included thinking big but starting small, and then introducing new behaviors to somewhat existing routines, such as early and frequent feedback from users of their software. This information helped to inform and prioritize the team's work—flipping their requirements questions from "Can we build it?" to "Should we build it?" Ironically, this resulted in the team delivering less, but a system that was used more by the users who helped them co-create it.

Spine Continues to Unlearn and Evolve

While Andrew and his team were working on Spine 2, Andrew's boss came up to him and said, "How do you fancy doing another project on top of this?" The project turned out to be Secondary Uses Service (SUS), which among other things supports the payments and commissioning of work in the secondary care environment.

Spine 2 went live in August 2014. The identity and access management service and the SUS went live in February 2015 without any issues whatsoever—no outages. The transition from Spine to Spine 2 was so seamless that two weeks after the release, people didn't even realize that they were running on the new service and were saying, "You are obviously late with the Spine 2 release. When will it be?" The cost savings have been considerable for the NHS. Says Andrew:

> We are saving £26 million a year on all the various Spine systems. BT have on their websites that it cost them 15,000 man-years to build Spine 1. It took us just 100 man-years to build Spine 2. And we did it with a small group of people with a dedicated mission working on what really mattered to our users.

The extraordinary results didn't end there. Spine 1 cost more than £50 million a year to run, handling 22 million messages per day sent between thousands of care organizations, ranging from large urban hospitals to small GP surgeries in remote rural areas. System shortfalls, instabilities, and crashes left users frustrated.

Spine 2 handles 45 million messages per day and accesses more than 2 billion records. Release costs are less than 0.1 percent of previous release costs, the system has been 99.999 percent available since going live, and it takes a total team of just 30 people to run it. Spine 2 has significantly reduced response times, giving the NHS back 750 working hours per day to help healthcare patients.[2]

As Andrew clearly demonstrated, you can do amazing things with a small, dedicated, cross-functional team whose members are clear on what their customers want, work in small batches, and ship the product in an iterative and adaptive manner. He found a variety of ways to drive the team toward the desired outcomes, using the constraints of the failing system to help it unlearn. According to Andrew, he would point to a deadline and say, "Beyond this date we will not have a Spine service unless we do something about it." That drove the organization and detractors to focus on the desired outcomes that needed to be achieved within the available schedule. You can stoke existential crisis or survival anxiety by highlighting the limited amount of time your team has. This is much the same approach that Drew used at Capital One to drive change in that company's systems, and that Andy Grove sensed as strategic inflection points at Intel. However, the key to unlocking endless experimentation, growth, and impact is to reduce learning anxiety within your organization.

Safety Scales the Cycle of Unlearning

To a large degree, Andrew believed that one of his most important responsibilities as a manager was to protect his team from the larger organization. His instruction to the team was to get on with their work, and he would make sure they had what they needed in order to deliver. It is absolutely crucial for any leader to protect the team, particularly when those above you in the organization are wedded to the old ways and fear doing something different than the status quo, even when the status quo is no longer working. Andrew could count on the protection of *his* boss at the time, Rob Shaw, who now serves as Health and Social Care Information Centre's deputy chief executive.

If you want to unlearn why innovation initiatives struggle in your organization, ask the people doing innovative work who helped make them successful and who provides the air cover that enables them to break through and achieve extraordinary results. Then support them. While air cover is not absolutely necessary to engage in the Cycle of Unlearning, it is a factor that creates the safety required for it to scale more quickly.

Sometimes the constraint is a timeline. Sometimes it's a budget. Sometimes you're going to go out of business because a competitor is releasing a new product. These constraints and downward pressure are often a catalyst to unlearn. While all these situations are pivotal moments to unlearn, the ideal state is not to be in a situation triggered by existential threats or crises, and instead adopt the practice of unlearning regularly—*habitually*.

With ongoing, deliberate practice, every one of us can leverage unlearning instinctively and use it intentionally—not just when there is no other alternative or option. We can then develop a capability to solve any challenge or cease any opportunity we face simply by unlearning what is holding us back, relearning new behaviors to address it, and break through and leap ahead. This unique capability is what enables leaders to continually find new and higher levels of performance—often beyond what they initially thought possible—within themselves, their teams, and their organizations.

12

Conclusion

You can't go back and change the beginning, but you can start where you are and change the ending.
—C. S. Lewis

'm excited to see how Serena Williams applies the Cycle of Unlearning to her next challenge either on or off the court. I sense she has the system in place to achieve whatever she sets her sights on, be it breaking Margaret Court's record of 24 individual Grand Slam titles, launching new businesses, or more.

I also have to wonder if the Cycle of Unlearning that the small Disney team adopted as it developed and rolled out its innovative new MagicBand in a secluded corner of Walt Disney World hasn't leaked out to the rest of the company's Parks and Resorts organization. Based on the most recent financial results of the Walt Disney Company, I have good reason to believe they have.

Overall, Disney's financial performance for 2017 was extremely disappointing for investors and top management alike, with a 1 percent decline in revenue from 2016 to 2017 (from $55.6 billion to $55.1 billion) and a 6 percent drop in operating income (from $15.7 billion to $14.8 billion). In fact, every major business segment except for one underperformed in 2017. From 2016 to 2017, Consumer Products and

Interactive Media revenue declined 13 percent (from $5.5 billion to $4.8 billion), Studio Entertainment revenue declined 11 percent (from $9.4 billion to $8.4 billion), and revenue for Media Networks dropped 1 percent (from $23.7 billion to $23.5 billion).[1]

The one shining star? Parks and Resorts.

While the revenues of every other segment decreased from 2016 to 2017, the revenue for Parks and Resorts increased 8 percent—from $17.0 billion to $18.4 billion. And operating income increased at an even greater clip, jumping 14 percent from 2016 to 2017 ($3.3 billion to $3.8 billion).[2]

While I cannot directly attribute the stellar results posted by Parks and Resorts for 2017 solely to the prompt provided by the MagicBands team, I suspect that as team members moved on to other parts of the organization, they brought the Cycle of Unlearning along with them. Disney chairman and CEO Bob Iger personally approved the MagicBands project, and he provided its leadership team with the remit to unlearn to achieve extraordinary results. Iger could clearly see the benefit of this new way of working with each small step the team took, and he championed it. This caused a ripple effect that swept across the Parks and Resorts business segment, and I believe someday it will flow throughout the entirety of the Disney organization—lifting it to even greater success in the future.

In the case of IAG—the parent company of Aer Lingus, British Airways, Iberia, LEVEL, Vueling, Avios Group Limited and IAG Cargo—I know the team of six Catapult leaders returned to their companies to champion the Cycle of Unlearning with new ways of working and to provide coaching to others throughout the organization to make an impact and contribute toward their extraordinary results.

Numerous other executives and leaders inspired by their stories have joined me in ExecCamps to break their models and reinvent their businesses and themselves. From airports to telcos, banks to healthcare companies, and more, the leaders of tomorrow don't fear the future but are instead inventing it. It's inspiring to work with these leaders in such uncomfortable, uncertain, and unknown domains.

Ultimately, the desired outcome of adopting the Cycle of Unlearning is to shift how we think, perceive, and experience the world; to gather new information in new ways that are no longer constrained by our past successes; and to use that information to improve our decision making and actions. When we unlearn, we relearn a system of effectiveness. The purpose is to question our assumptions—as Eleanor Roosevelt cautioned, never mistaking knowledge for wisdom—and challenge our understanding to gain valuable lessons from what we have learned and adapt.

The telco executive team unlearned their mobile phone strategy thanks to a $200 pre-paid credit card and the experience of their own service as a customer. The executive from IAG unlearned how to co-create outstanding products by listening to the feedback of his customer. The bank leadership team unlearned their incentive structure and its unintended consequences to achieve their desired organizational-level outcomes.

The question is what behaviors and mindsets currently limit your capabilities? Will *you* unlearn in order to relearn new behaviors and break through to extraordinary results?

Unlearning is a system that requires dedicated time and focus to achieve mastery, but the effort is well worth it. It is important to step slightly outside our comfort zone—our toes barely touching the bottom as we go out of our depth—to seek opportunities to experience new ways of thinking, acting, and working. With deliberate practice, reflection, and repetition, you will improve your performance, understand new patterns, and build that mastery. You will reinforce your lessons learned, coach, mentor, and bring others along the journey. You will be able to design systems of work that include and enhance virtuous cycles of unlearning to have profound impact on your customers, colleagues, and yourself.

The most powerful part of the Cycle of Unlearning is the simple fact that there will always be more to unlearn, more to relearn, and more breakthroughs to take both you and your organization to the next level. Our world will continue to increase in speed, complexity, and innovation at an exponential rate, and organizations—and the people who lead them—must keep up to survive, and get ahead to thrive.

As Chinese philosopher Lao Tzu said, "To attain knowledge, add things every day. To attain wisdom, remove things every day." These words are just as true today as they were 1,500 years ago.

Leading Culture Change Means Changing Yourself Before Others

Naysayers will tell you it's not possible, citing the size of the challenge, the belief that people won't change, and the many obstacles that will get in your way and stop you. They'll raise endless reasons why it wouldn't work, couldn't work, or has been tried before. Turn these obstacles into opportunities. Feed them into the Cycle of Unlearning and break through.

Many erroneously believe that creating new behaviors requires first changing the mindset—that if we tell people to start thinking differently, they will start acting differently. Nothing could be further from the truth.

Unlearning does not lead with words; it leads with *action*. This means thinking big, but making small steps toward the outcome we desire. And it also means leading the unlearning ourselves, thereby providing the example for others on our team and in our organization to follow by adapting our own behavior. While objections are indeed challenges, the most serious barriers are to be found in organizational culture, leadership, and strategy—all of which can be affected by unlearning outdated and legacy behaviors in order to relearn better behaviors and break through. You tackle that challenge by starting with yourself, not trying to fix others. Model the behaviors you wish to see, and others will follow.

By unlearning the way we behave, our actions begin to inform the way we observe, experience, and eventually see the world. This new perspective of seeing and experiencing the world differently impacts the way we think about it. People do not change their mental models of the world by speaking about it; they need to experience the change to believe, feel, and see evidence of it.

Remember, *unlearning* is the process of letting go, reframing, and moving away from once-useful mindsets and acquired behaviors that were effective in the past, but now limit our success. It's not forgetting, removing, or discarding knowledge or experience; it's the conscious act of letting go of outdated information and actively engaging in taking in new information to inform effective decision making and action.

Bringing About Unlearning in a Large Organization

The experience of the Disney MagicBand team is very similar to the experience of the six senior IAG leaders who were pulled out of their organization for eight weeks to unlearn. Just as Disney knew that it couldn't rely on one-day innovation off-sites or massive multiyear transformational programs to create extraordinary outcomes or any lasting behavior or mindset breakthroughs, so too did the leadership of IAG realize that it would have to do something quite different than it had been doing to drive innovation and extraordinary results. This something different was to engage in the Cycle of Unlearning.

Similarly, Capital One knew that by reinventing their ways of working—and themselves—they could make a tremendous difference in the organization's outcomes. By taking on challenges outside their comfort zones and knowledge thresholds to discover, experiment with, and use new methods, tools, and techniques, they would enable employees at all levels of the organization to break free of fixed behaviors and myopic mindsets.

For Jeff Bezos, at Amazon, it's always Day One. When employees move past Day One, they become complacent and fearful, relying more on the comfort of the status quo instead of constantly seeking new frontiers and courageously leaning into the discomfort of the unknown. The former is the pathway to organizational decline and death. The latter is the pathway to greatness.

If your purpose is leading unlearning in your team or organization, take inspiration from them. Think big and start small. Identify what needs to be unlearned and seek out the right people and leadership support. Demonstrate that the company's own people can achieve extraordinary results and their own aspirations and outcomes, with new ways of working. Share your vision, mistakes, and actions. Model the new behaviors you wish to see.

Why Most People Will Remain in Mediocrity

Most people will never put themselves in uncomfortable situations or embrace uncertainty and the unknown. Why not? Because the pull toward mediocrity is too strong. Much of the thinking is small-minded with little action. Many people are overly concerned with beating their personal rivals, usually through manipulation and politics. Rarely will these people achieve extraordinary results. Instead, focus your time and effort on what you can do to grow and have impact yourself.

As you consider the many different challenges, aspirations, and outcomes you want to set for yourself, I believe the most important ones are experiential learning and personal transformation. I have found that if you're always chasing success, it will constantly elude you. But if you always prioritize incredible personal growth, impact, and paradigm-shifting experiences, success will gravitate toward you as if you were a magnet.

So, choose not to be mediocre. Choose a life of greatness—at work, at home, in your community, and in the world. Remember: Think big, but start small. Take the tiny steps to achieve the outcomes you desire. Step by step, you can and will achieve all that you want—maybe even more than you can imagine.

Recognize when your behaviors and mindset aren't working or living up to your expectations or could be better. Take action by trying a different approach without a guaranteed successful outcome. This takes something very special: It takes *courage* and a willingness to be *vulnerable* to the possibility of failure. It is at this precise intersection that true greatness occurs.

One Thing You Can Do Tomorrow to Start Your Own Cycle of Unlearning

As we reach the final pages of this book, the one thing I most want you to remember is that the Cycle of Unlearning begins with *you*. Think about what you want to unlearn for yourself and commit to start. There is no ideal state or moment or situation, and waiting for existential threats or crises is not fun. Instead, adopt the practice of unlearning intentionally and habitually as we do breathing and living. As Jeff Bezos says, "There is no Day Two—*every* day is Day One."

Don't wait a moment longer to define the aspiration or outcome you most want to accomplish. Start tomorrow, or even better, right now—it's easy to do!

Write down the aspiration or outcome you want to achieve, then quantify and constrain it. Ask someone on your team, a colleague, or friend, "On a scale of 1 to 10, how well do you think I am doing at _____ (the aspiration or outcome you want to achieve)?"

This technique was taught to me by executive coach Sabrina Braham.[3] She highlights that the human brain can't adequately calibrate typical qualitative feedback responses such as "poor," "fair," "good," and "excellent." Those words don't have any precise meanings for us. However, when someone gives us quantitative feedback—a percentage, rate, or ratio—the brain immediately understands, and we know where to focus our effort. For example, "You're a 6 out of 10"—in essence, 60 percent of the way toward your aspiration or outcome.

Listen to what your collaborator, co-creator, or customer has to say. Ask them what behaviors are helping you get there or holding you back. Ask them how you could get half a point better. What is the one small step you could take to improve, get better results, and unlearn?

Think about the first step you'll take as a tiny habit that you can introduce to your routine the next time you do it. Check back with them later to see if you've actually achieved the breakthrough you're looking for—not only with them, but with your own way of seeing the world differently. And then start to build virtuous cycles that build your effectiveness and lead to increasingly better outcomes with each iteration and Cycle of Unlearning you complete.

I can guarantee that if you take that approach, you'll get extraordinary results.

Acknowledgments

No worthwhile work is enacted by a sole individual. I've reflected many times that to go fast you go alone, but to go far means going together. Many people have joined me at various stages of this journey, prompting and pushing me in better directions. This book is a result of their belief and bets on me.

To Qiu Yi, my wife and greatest supporter. Your selflessness astounds me; your kindness inspires me to be better, develop, and grow. To Oscar, our newborn son, for keeping me on time and giving me as much energy as the sleep you took away. To my parents for all you gave up to give me more. I hope I can be half the role model you've been for me. To my brothers and sisters, nephews, and niece—you're never far from my thoughts, no matter the distance or day. To Swe-Nge for making the finishing line a possibility. I thank you all.

To Aaron Gette, Adrian Cockcroft, Andrew Meyer, Andy Clay Shefter, Ash Pal, Ben Kappler, Ben Williams, Bill Higgins, BJ Fogg, Breanden Beneschott, Bridget Samburg, Catherine Dungan, Chivas Nambiar, Chris Lichti, David Bland, David Marquet, Dean Bosche, Derek O'Brien, Drew Firment, Ed Hoffman, Eric Ries, Fin Goulding, Gavin Harmon, Glenn Morgan, Heather Arnett, Holly Hester-Reilly, Jake Knapp, JB Brown, Jeff Gothelf, Jeff Leap, Jeff Reihl, Jeffrey Liker, Jenn Bennett, Jerome Bonhomme, Joanne Molesky, Jody Mulkey, Joel Goldberg, John Marcante, Jonny Scheinder, Jora Gill, Josh Seiden, Karen Martin, Katri Harra-Salonen, Kris Harrison, Lea Hickman, Lee Ditiangkin, Loretta Breuning, Marcin Kwiatkowski, Martin Ericksson, Mary Poppendieck, Matthew May, Max Griffths, Melissa Perri, Mike Rother, Niall O'Reilly, Nik Willets, Nils Stamm, Noelle Eder, Reshma Shaikh, Richard Lennox, Rob Nail, Ron Garrett, Sabrina Braham, Sarah Barlett, Scott Turnquest, Sean Murphy, Stephane Kasriel, Stephanie Weldy, Stephen Orban, Stephen Scott, Stuart Wilson, Teresa Torres, Terren Peterson, Thaniya Keereepart, Tom Poppendieck, and Yen Chang for your contributions, reviews, and feedback. Your inspiration and insights have made this book better than I could have hoped for. Thank you all for your patience and your time. This work is as much yours as mine. I like building the future with you all.

To the team at McGraw-Hill, especially Casey Ebro for her willingness to champion this book and the excitement to make it a reality.

To Esmond Harmsworth for guiding me through the publishing world and finding the right fit.

And finally, to my writing compadre and friend, Peter Economy. Put simply, this book would not exist without you. Your guidance, humor, and passion for this project always exceeded mine when I needed it to. I've unlearned and relearned much from you. Thanks for all the breakthroughs. I already look forward to our next adventure writing together.

Notes

Introduction: The Remarkable Power of Unlearning

1. http://www.nytimes.com/2012/05/30/sports/tennis/2012-french-open
    -serena-williams-ousted-in-first-round.html

Chapter 1: Why Unlearn?

1. http://www.cnbc.com/2017/01/28/professional-tennis-is-older-than-its
    -ever-been.html

2. http://www.newsweek.com/2016/07/01/patrick-mouratoglou-serena
    -williams-coach-471758.html

3. https://www.telegraph.co.uk/sport/tennis/wimbledon/2316311/Serena
    -shows-strength-to-win.html

4. https://www.usatoday.com/story/sports/tennis/2013/09/02/us-open
    -2013-serena-williams-patrick-mouratoglou-partnership/2755659/

5. http://www.newsweek.com/2016/07/01/patrick-mouratoglou-serena
    -williams-coach-471758.html

6. http://www.newsweek.com/2016/07/01/patrick-mouratoglou-serena
    -williams-coach-471758.html

7. https://www.tennisconsult.com/interview-patrick-mouratoglou/ and https:
    //www.mouratoglou.com/site/uploaded/ckeditor/files/Tennis_School
    _EN_2018.pdf

8. http://www.espn.com/espnw/news-commentary/article/13616431/us
    -open-how-serena-williams-found-new-level-success-coach-patrick
    -mouratoglou

9. http://www.espn.com/tennis/story/_/id/18445144/serena-williams-coach -makes-clear-2017-all-grand-slams

10. http://www.espn.com/espnw/news-commentary/article/13142903/how -serena-williams-mastered-art-comeback

11. http://www.mathistopheles.co.uk/maths/how-much-is-a-set-worth/

12. https://ftw.usatoday.com/2018/05/serena-williams-french-open-stats

13. https://www.instagram.com/p/BiW668QlUpA/?taken-by=serenawilliams

14. http://www.newsweek.com/serena-williams-pregnancy-2017-australian -open-586582

15. Baron de Montesquieu, Considerations on the Causes of the Greatness of the Romans and Their Decline (1734) http://www.constitution.org/cm/ ccgrd_l.htm

16. Peter Senge, The Fifth Discipline: The Art & Practice of the Learning Organization, Doubleday (1990) pp. 57–67

17. Hedberg, B. How organizations learn and unlearn. In P. C. Nystrom & W. H. Starbuck (Eds), Handbook of organizational design, Vol. 1. Oxford: Oxford University Press, 1981, pp. 3–27

Chapter 2: How to Unlearn

1. https://hbr.org/2016/10/why-leadership-training-fails-and-what-to-do -about-it

2. Edmondson, A.; Lei, Z. (2014). "Psychological Safety: The History, Renaissance, and Future of an Interpersonal Construct." *Annual Review of Organizational Psychology and Organizational Behavior*, **1**: 23–43. doi:10 .1146/annurev-orgpsych-031413-091305

3. http://www.iagpress.com/phoenix.zhtml?c=240949&p=aboutoverview

4. http://www.iairgroup.com/phoenix.zhtml?c=240949&p=irol-newsArticle &ID=2234865

5. https://onemileatatime.boardingarea.com/2017/03/19/Level-airline -tickets/

6. https://www.theguardian.com/commentisfree/2016/apr/04/uncertainty -stressful-research-neuroscience

Chapter 3: Unlearning the Obstacles to Unlearning

1. https://www.forbes.com/sites/brucerogers/2016/01/07/why-84-of -companies-fail-at-digital-transformation/#f7f5a61397bd

2. https://www.ted.com/talks/ken_robinson_says_schools_kill_creativity/ transcript

3. https://www.ncbi.nlm.nih.gov/pmc/articles/PMC1765804/pdf/v013p0ii22.pdf

4. https://www.ncbi.nlm.nih.gov/pmc/articles/PMC1765804/pdf/v013p0ii22.pdf

5. http://www.bizjournals.com/orlando/news/2016/11/10/the-walt-disney-co-reports-record-revenue-theme.html

6. https://www.wired.com/2015/03/disney-magicband/

7. https://en.wikiquote.org/wiki/Walt_Disney

Chapter 4: Unlearn

1. Paul Reps and Nyogen Senzaki, *Zen Flesh Zen Bones: A Collection of Zen and Pre-Zen Writings*, Tuttle Publishing (1998) p. 23.

2. Brené Brown, Rising Strong: How the Ability to Reset Transforms the Way We Live, Love, Parent, and Lead, Spiegel & Grau (2015) p. 5.

Chapter 5: Relearn

1. https://www.themuse.com/advice/how-much-time-do-we-spend-in-meetings-hint-its-scary

2. https://hbr.org/2002/03/the-anxiety-of-learning

3. http://womensrunning.competitor.com/2017/02/training-tips/training-plans/go-couch-marathon-training-plan_71868

4. https://health.usnews.com/health-news/blogs/eat-run/articles/2015-12-29/why-80-percent-of-new-years-resolutions-fail

Chapter 6: Breakthrough

1. https://www.usatoday.com/story/sports/nfl/2014/07/30/metrics-sensor-shoulder-pads-zebra-speed-tracking/13382443/

2. https://mindsetonline.com/whatisit/about/

3. https://hbr.org/2002/03/the-anxiety-of-learning

4. https://hbr.org/2002/03/the-anxiety-of-learning

5. https://www.smithsonianmag.com/innovation/thomas-edisons-house-wizardy-180952108/

6. http://www.openculture.com/2014/12/leonardo-da-vincis-to-do-list-circa-1490-is-much-cooler-than-yours.html

7. https://www.fastcompany.com/3063846/why-these-tech-companies-keep-running-thousands-of-failed

8. https://www.fastcompany.com/3067455/why-amazon-is-the-worlds -most-innovative-company-of-2017

9. https://www.youtube.com/watch?time_continue=610&v=dxk8b9rSKOo

Chapter 7: Unlearning Management

1. http://processcoaching.com/fourstages.html

2. Gary Hamel, *The Future of Management*, Harvard Business Review Press (2007) p. 255.

3. Peter Drucker, *Managing for Results*, Collins (1993) p. 222.

4. Peter Drucker, *Managing for Results*, Collins (1993) p. 222.

5. http://awealthofcommonsense.com/2016/04/napoleons-corporal/

6. Marquet uses the world "boss" and "worker" to denote hierarchy.

7. http://davidmarquet-com.3dcartstores.com/Ladder-of-Leadership-Wallet -Cards-Starter-Pack-bundle-of-25_p_50.html

8. https://www.flickr.com/photos/benarent/2195470990

9. https://positivepsychologyprogram.com/mihaly-csikszentmihalyi-father -of-flow/

10. http://www.autonews.com/article/20140805/OEM01/140809892/ toyota-cutting-the-fabled-andon-cord-symbol-of-toyota-way

11. https://www.cnbc.com/2018/02/01/aws-earnings-q4-2017.html

12. https://www.amazon.jobs/principles

13. http://phx.corporate-ir.net/phoenix.zhtml?c=97664&p=irol-news Article&ID=2329885

14. Ray Dalio, *Principles: Life and Work*, Simon and Schuster (2017).

Chapter 8: Unlearning with Customers

1. John Legere, "T-Mobile's CEO on Winning Market Share by Trash-Talking Rivals," *Harvard Business Review* (January-February 2017).

2. https://barryoreilly.com/2014/08/06/why-we-carry-watermelons/

3. http://quotes.deming.org/authors/W._Edwards_Deming/quote/10201

4. http://www.bain.com/bainweb/pdfs/cms/hotTopics/closingdeliverygap .pdf

5. John Legere, "T-Mobile's CEO on Winning Market Share by Trash-Talking Rivals," *Harvard Business Review* (January-February 2017).

6. https://newsroom.t-mobile.com/news-and-blogs/tmus-q4-2017-earnings .htm

7. https://www.inc.com/justin-bariso/elon-musk-takes-customer-complaint-on-twitter-from-idea-to-execution-in-6-days.html

8. https://www.cnbc.com/2017/09/18/elon-musk-tweets-an-unhappy-tesla-customer.html

Chapter 9: Unlearning with People and Organizations

1. Diane Vaughan (4 January 2016). *The Challenger Launch Decision: Risky Technology, Culture, and Deviance at NASA*, Enlarged Edition. University of Chicago Press. pp.30–1. ISBN 978-0-226-34696-0.

2. https://www.nytimes.com/2016/02/28/magazine/what-google-learned-from-its-quest-to-build-the-perfect-team.html?smid=pl-share

3. https://www.nasa.gov/specials/dor2017/

4. https://www.nasa.gov/specials/dor2017/

5. https://www.researchgate.net/publication/249631357_The_Nature_and__Need_for_Informal_Learning

6. http://www.richardswanson.com/textbookresources/wp-content/uploads/2013/08/TBAD-r9b-Watkins.-DLOQ-Demonstrating-Value.pdf

7. https://www.ncbi.nlm.nih.gov/pmc/articles/PMC4326496/table/Tab2/

Chapter 10: Unlearning Incentives

1. https://www.cnbc.com/id/29740717

2. https://hbr.org/2013/10/doubts-about-pay-for-performance-in-health-care

3. https://www.nytimes.com/2018/02/10/business/economy/bonus-pay.html

4. http://fortune.com/2015/09/02/ceo-pay-flatter-salaries-but-bigger-bonuses/

5. https://www.washingtonpost.com/news/on-leadership/wp/2018/04/11/median-ceo-pay-for-the-100-largest-companies-reached-a-record-15-7-million-in-2017/

6. http://news.gallup.com/opinion/gallup/224012/dismal-employee-engagement-sign-global-mismanagement.aspx

7. http://lexicon.ft.com/term?term=principal/agent-problem

8. https://en.wikipedia.org/wiki/Principal%E2%80%93agent_problem

9. http://money.cnn.com/2017/08/31/investing/wells-fargo-fake-accounts/index.html

10. https://www.nytimes.com/2016/09/09/business/dealbook/wells-fargo -fined-for-years-of-harm-to-customers.html

11. https://www.forbes.com/sites/victorlipman/2014/11/04/what-motivates -employees-to-go-the-extra-mile-study-offers-surprising-answer/#1ef59 37ca055

Chapter 11: Unlearning with Business and Product Innovation

1. https://digital.nhs.uk/spine

2. https://www.yorkshireeveningpost.co.uk/news/leeds-based-spine-digital -system-is-backbone-of-nhs-1-8073182

Chapter 12: Conclusion

1. https://thewaltdisneycompany.com/walt-disney-company-reports-fourth -quarter-full-year-earnings-fiscal-2017/

2. https://thewaltdisneycompany.com/walt-disney-company-reports-fourth -quarter-full-year-earnings-fiscal-2017/

3. https://www.womensleadershipsuccess.com/feedback-for-results/

Index

About the Author

Barry O'Reilly is a business advisor, entrepreneur, and author who has pioneered the intersection of business model innovation, product development, organizational design, and culture transformation. He works with business leaders and teams from global organizations that seek to invent the future, not fear it. Every day, Barry helps many of the world's leading companies, from disruptive startups to Fortune 500 behemoths, break the vicious cycles that hold them back by enabling a culture of experimentation and teaching them how to unlock the insights required for better decision making, higher performance, and greater results.

Barry is a coauthor of the international bestseller *Lean Enterprise: How High Performance Organizations Innovate at Scale*—included in the Eric Ries series, and a *Harvard Business Review* must-read for CEOs and business leaders. He is an internationally sought-after speaker and a frequent writer for and contributor to *The Economist*, *Strategy+Business*, and *MIT Sloan Management Review*.

A faculty member at Singularity University, Barry advises and contributes to Singularity's executive and accelerator programs in San Francisco and throughout the globe. He is the founder of ExecCamp, the entrepreneurial experience for executives, and the management consultancy Antennae. His mission is to help purposeful, technology-led businesses innovate at scale.

Read Barry's blog at www.barryoreilly.com and connect with him on Twitter @barryoreilly.